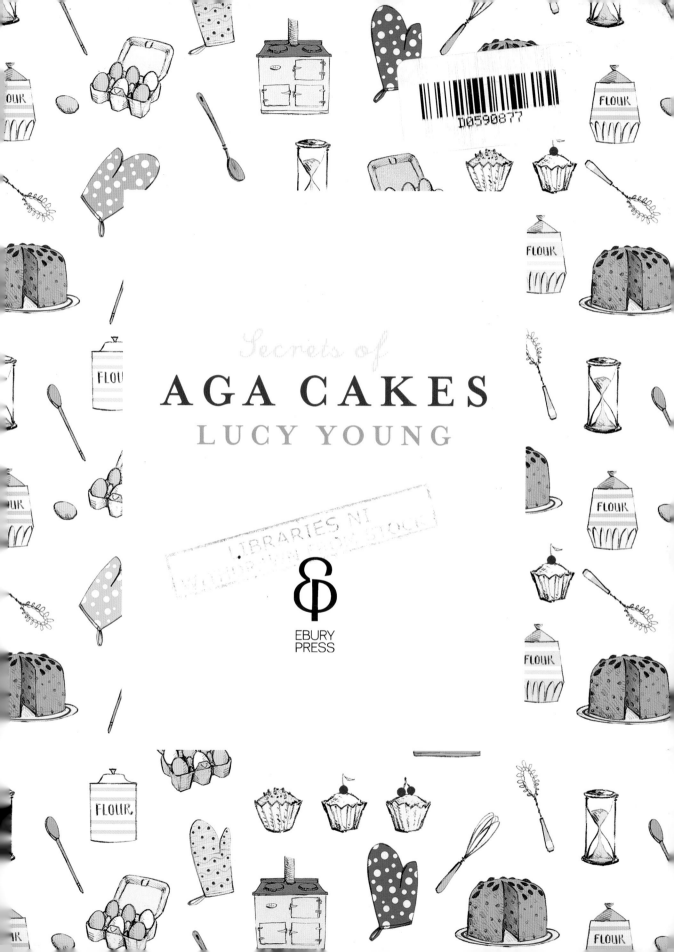

Secrets of

AGA CAKES

LUCY YOUNG

EBURY
PRESS

1 3 5 7 9 10 8 6 4 2

Published in 2007 by Ebury Press, an imprint of Ebury
Publishing

Ebury Publishing is a division of the Random House Group

Text © Lucy Young 2007

Photography by Will Heap

All images © Ebury Press 2007

Lucy Young has asserted her right under the Copyright,
Designs and Patents Act 1988 to be identified as the author
of this work.

The Random House Group Limited Reg. No. 954009

Addresses for companies within the Random House Group
can be found at www.randomhouse.co.uk

A CIP catalogue record for this book is available from the
British Library

The Random House Group makes every effort to ensure
that the papers used in our books are made from trees that
have been legally sourced from well-managed and credibly
certified forests. Our paper procurement policy can be
found on www.randomhouse.co.uk

Editor: Emma Callery

Designer: Estuary English

Illustrations: Mary Claire Smith

Photographer: Will Heap

Food stylist: Alice Hart

Props stylist: Rachel Jukes

Printed and bound in Italy by Printer Trento S.r.l.

ISBN: 9780091922412

To buy books by your favourite authors and register for
offers visit www.rbooks.co.uk

Contents

Mary Berry

This wonderful book is the first glossy Aga Book to be totally dedicated to cake baking. It is crammed full of every sort of cake, biscuit, bun, teabread and traditional cake that you can think of. I have written many cake books, but never one with Aga instructions, so I especially welcome this book as the bible for all Aga cake bakers.

No one has more practical experience with the Aga and baking than Lucy — I should know, she has been by my side for some 17 years. Together we have been running Aga Workshops at Watercroft and baking has always been an important part of each day. Sometimes baking in the Aga can be tricky, and it is specialised, but we have cracked it! Lucy has always been keen to try new, modern, young ideas as well as the traditional classics and this book has them all.

I think I have tasted just about every recipe in this book! Lucy would create and test them at home and bring them in. We would also often freeze them and serve them for garden open days for the National Garden Scheme charity, so they have been devoured by very many people. Yes, these recipes have been tried and tested many times — they are not just recipes on paper.

In this book, Lucy gently holds your hand through each step, sharing her baking skills with you. There is no technical jargon, just how to make, how to bake and how to present beautifully — follow all these instructions and her secrets and you will have success every time.

This book is certainly top of the wish list for all my Aga friends who are always on the phone asking us for advice! Hope you enjoy, it certainly is a book to be proud of.

Introduction

This is the first cake baking book for Aga owners, specifically giving you recipes for cakes, buns, biscuits and muffins — all the lovely things you want to make, but have found tricky to make in the Aga. I am often asked at demonstrations, 'When are you writing an Aga cake book?', and the answer is NOW! The recipes in this book are therefore all sweet recipes — this book teaches the Aga technique and makes cake baking simple.

Recipes range from the classic to the contemporary, with over 100 choices for both the keen cake baker and the complete beginner. There are ideas for all occasions, or simply fast cakes for the busy person, and even recipes that children will enjoy making themselves.

All the recipes have Aga and conventional cooking instructions, plus I've given lots of 'secrets' and tips that you can use to improve your cake-making. Enjoy!

AGA CAKE BAKING TIPS

Here are a few tips on using your Aga, together with some cake baking hints. These will help make your recipes perfect, stunning and delicious every time! It is important to follow the recipes accurately, so use the correct measurements, tins and position in the Aga. On these pages you will also find tips on knowing when a cake or biscuit is cooked and how to store and freeze them.

THE AGA

- Boiling plate is the left top plate.
- Simmering plate is the right top plate.
- Two-oven Aga: the top oven is the roasting oven and the bottom oven is the simmering oven.
- Three-oven Aga: the top oven is the roasting oven, bottom right is the simmering oven and bottom left is the baking oven.

- Four-oven Aga: top right is the roasting oven, top left is the simmering oven, bottom right is the baking oven and bottom left is the warming oven.

- The grid shelf is the ridged shelf that comes with the Aga and stays in the oven.

- The cold sheet is the sheet that comes free with your Aga and is a flat metal sheet the size of the ovens. This stays out of the Aga so it is always cold and is used to blank off the heat from the top of the oven to prevent the contents from burning.

- When a 'runner' is mentioned in a recipe, e.g. slide onto the second set of runners, they are counted from the top.

- A small Aga roasting tin is half the size of the large Aga roasting tin, so a recipe for a small tin can be doubled to fit into the big tin.

General Aga tips

- For beginners, cook shallow cakes with short cooking times.

- Two-oven Aga owners: bake on the grid shelf on the floor of the roasting oven with the cold sheet on the second set of runners above. This lowers the temperature of the oven, preventing the cake from burning. Very deep cakes need to be baked in an Aga Cake Baker.

- Three- and four-oven Aga owners: bake in the baking oven, with the option of using the cold sheet if the cake is getting too brown.

- Most cakes are simple to bake as long as baked in the correct oven, correct tin, correct position and for the right length of time.

- Use the correct size tin stated in the recipe; if not, this will affect the cooking time.

- Rich fruit cakes are baked in the simmering oven with great success.

- Drop scones and Welsh cakes do not need a griddle pan as they can be cooked directly on the greased simmering plate.

- Biscuits can be tricky to bake because of their high proportion of sugar, so watch carefully.

- If making a whisked sponge, warm the sugar in the simmering or warming oven to give more bulk when whisking.

- Do not open the door too often at the start of baking. Also, always close the door gently, do not slam it.

Making cakes and biscuits

- Weigh in either imperial or metric, do not mix the two.

- When making a cake by hand, use a large bowl and beat with a wooden spoon or plastic spatula until completely mixed and smooth.

- When making cakes in a processor, use the metal blade and whiz until just mixed. Do not over-whiz otherwise the cake will lose its volume and will not rise in the oven, resulting in a flat cake.

- Do not add too much baking powder. Use as stated in the recipe otherwise the cake will rise too high in the oven and, once removed, will collapse, causing the cake to have a dip in the middle.

- All eggs used in the recipes are large. It is always better to use them at room temperature for whisked sponges as this makes whisking quicker.

- Use caster sugar rather than granulated sugar in a cake, as granulated sugar will give a speckled effect on the top of the cake.

- If using fruit in syrup, e.g. cherries and ginger, be sure to wash and dry well otherwise the fruit will sink to the bottom of the cake.

- Use baking margarine from the fridge. If using butter, bring to room temperature until soft, but not too melted so it separates, otherwise the butter will not mix in well to the other ingredients.

- Do not buy a spread to bake with, buy a margarine suitable for baking; look on the back of the tub for a high fat content as a high fat content is important for cake baking and gives the best results. Using a spread will result in a flat cake.

- Use non-stick baking parchment to line tins. Grease underneath the paper so it sticks easily to the tin.

- To grease a tin, use soft margarine or butter, not oil.

To test when cooked

- A sponge cake should be well risen, golden brown and shrinking away from the sides of the tin. Press the centre of the cake with your finger. If the sponge springs back, the cake is cooked; if the fingerprint stays indented, it needs longer in the oven.

- For a fruit cake, insert a skewer into the centre of the cake. If it comes out clean, the cake is cooked.

- Biscuits will be slightly darker around the edge and the centre will be soft but not oily. Biscuits become crisp once cooled.

Cooked cakes and biscuits

- When a sponge cake is cooked, remove from the oven, leave in the tin and run around the edge of the cake and the tin with a palette knife to release the cake from the sides of the tin. Set aside to cool.

- Once cool, invert onto a tea towel on a board or cooling rack and tip over again the right way up onto a cooling rack and leave until stone cold. If you turn a warm cake onto an uncovered cooling rack, the rack will leave marks in the top of the cake.

- If you are leaving a cake for a long time before icing, leave the cake tins upturned over the cake to retain the moisture and prevent the cake from drying out.

- After removing biscuits from the oven, leave them for about 10 minutes to firm up on the baking sheet. Carefully remove with a fish slice or palette knife onto a cooling rack to become completely cold.

STORING AND FREEZING

- Keep cooked cakes in a cake tin in a cool, dry place.

- If iced and the icing is made of cream or other dairy product, keep the cake covered in cling film in the fridge.

- Most cakes freeze well un-iced or iced — I advise freezing un-iced then ice on the day as this prevents the icing from losing its shine and freshness.

- Freeze a cold cake wrapped in cling film in a sealed plastic bag.

- Freeze cakes flat without putting anything on top of them.

- Keep and freeze biscuits in plastic containers, layered with kitchen paper. The paper absorbs the moisture and therefore prevents the biscuits from becoming soft.

- Some biscuits may need refreshing once frozen — arrange flat on a baking sheet in a single layer and refresh in the simmering oven for about 8–10 minutes.

- A dense fruit cake, such as a Christmas cake, can be wrapped in paper and foil and kept in the fridge or in a dry, cool place for up to six months.

ICING CAKES

- Whenever icing or filling a cake, the cake must be stone cold otherwise the icing will slide off the cake.

- Spreading the top and middle of a cake with jam keeps the cake moist and prevents the crumbs of the cake from mixing with the icing.

- Icing should be spreading consistency, so if the icing is heated, leave it to firm up a little before spreading. For piped icings, set aside until piping consistency.

- To coat the top of a cake, use a palette knife horizontally and vertically when coating the sides.

- Ice using a palette knife, it gives a smooth finish.

- When spreading a cake with a frosting or smooth rich icing, dip a palette knife in a jug of hot water, shake the knife to remove any drips and use to spread the icing. This will make spreading easier and give a smooth finish.

Simple cakes

Traybakes are the quickest and easiest cakes to make, they serve many people and are pretty foolproof – this chapter has lots of different ideas for traybakes and easy all-in-one cakes. They are ideal for the Aga as they are baked in the small and large roasting tins that come with every Aga. Each of the recipes in this chapter is made in the small Aga roasting tin, but if you want to make a recipe in the large Aga roasting tin for a birthday party or large family gathering, just double the quantities.

CHOCOLATE TRAYBAKE

This is definitely the quickest and easiest way to cook a quantity of cakes for a party. This quantity fits the small Aga roasting tin, double the quantities to fit the large roasting tin. It freezes well iced or un-iced.

- Cuts into 16 pieces

> 25 g (1 oz) cocoa powder
> 3 tbsp boiling water
> 225 g (8 oz) baking margarine, from the fridge
> 225 g (8 oz) caster sugar
> 300 g (10 oz) self-raising flour
> 2 tsp baking powder
> 4 eggs
> 2 tbsp milk

- For the ganache icing

> 150 g (5 oz) dark chocolate
> 1 x 200 ml pot full-fat crème fraîche
> Raspberry jam for spreading, warmed

You will need a small Aga roasting tin (or traybake tin measuring 30 x 23 cm/12 x 9 in), lined with foil and greased.

Measure the cocoa powder into a bowl and mix with the boiling water to give a smooth paste. Add the remaining ingredients to the bowl and beat well until smooth. Pour into the prepared tin.

TWO-OVEN AGA Slide the tin onto the grid shelf in the roasting oven with the cold shelf on the second set of runners. Bake for 25–30 minutes, until shrinking away from the sides of the tin and springy to the touch. Turn once during cooking.

THREE- AND FOUR-OVEN AGA Slide the tin onto the lowest set of runners in the baking oven and bake for about 20 minutes, until shrinking away from the sides of the tin and springy to the touch. If the cake is getting too brown, slide the cold sheet onto the second set of runners.

CONVENTIONAL OVEN Bake in a preheated oven (180°C/350°F/160°C Fan/Gas 4) for about 30 minutes.

Leave to cool in the tin.

For the icing, measure the chocolate and crème fraîche into a bowl and leave on the back of the Aga. Stir occasionally until all the chocolate has melted. (For a conventional oven, measure the chocolate and crème fraîche into a bowl and heat gently over a pan of simmering water, stirring until melted.) Set aside to thicken a little. When the cake has cooled, spread with warm raspberry jam and spread over the icing.

Secret

- Warming the jam makes it easier to spread over the cake. The easiest way to warm the jam to save heating in a pan is to sit the jar on the back of the Aga or in the simmering oven for about 10 minutes.

ICED LEMON TRAYBAKE

A classic lemon traybake with a wonderful lemony icing. During the summer we open Mary's garden for charity and serve this cake for tea, and it is always the most popular cake we do. It freezes well un-iced. (See the photograph on page 15.)

- Cuts into 16 pieces

> 225 g (8 oz) baking margarine, from the fridge
> 225 g (8 oz) caster sugar
> 300 g (10 oz) self-raising flour
> 2 tsp baking powder
> 4 eggs
> 4 tbsp milk
> Grated rind of 2 lemons

- For the icing

> 225 g (8 oz) icing sugar, sifted
> About 3 tbsp lemon juice

You will need a small Aga roasting tin (or traybake tin measuring 30 x 23 cm/12 x 9 in), lined with foil and greased.

Measure all the cake ingredients in a bowl and mix together until smooth. Pour into the prepared tin.

TWO-OVEN AGA Slide the tin onto the grid shelf on the floor of the roasting oven with the cold sheet on the second set of runners. Bake for 25–30 minutes, until golden brown and shrinking away from the sides of the tin and springy to the touch.

THREE- AND FOUR-OVEN AGA Slide the tin onto the lowest set of runners in the baking oven and bake for 25–30 minutes, until golden brown and shrinking away from the sides of the tin and springy to the touch. If the cake is getting too brown, slide the cold sheet onto the second set of runners.

CONVENTIONAL OVEN Bake in a preheated oven (180°C/350°F/160°C Fan/Gas 4) for about 30 minutes.

Leave to cool in the tin.

To make the icing, sieve the icing sugar over a bowl and mix in the lemon juice. Beat until smooth and then spread evenly over the cold cake and set aside to set.

Secret
- You can make cake mixtures like this by hand in a large bowl, beating well with a wooden spoon. Alternatively, make in a processor or a freestanding mixer, but be careful not to over-beat otherwise the cake will not rise successfully in the oven.

BANANA AND CHOCOLATE CHIP TRAYBAKE

I love the combination of banana and chocolate. In my first book I invented a recipe for banana and chocolate muffins, which were so popular, this traybake should go down well, too! It freezes well.

- Cuts into 16 pieces

> 175 g (6 oz) baking margarine, from the fridge
> 250 g (9 oz) caster sugar
> 350 g (12 oz) self-raising flour
> 2 tsp baking powder
> 4 eggs
> 3 ripe bananas, mashed with a fork
> 3 tbsp milk
> 75 g (3 oz) dark chocolate chips

You will need a small Aga roasting tin (or traybake tin measuring 30 x 23 cm/12 x 9 in), lined with foil and greased.

Measure all the cake ingredients together in a bowl and mix together until smooth. Pour into the prepared tin.

TWO-OVEN AGA Slide the tin onto the lowest set of runners in the roasting oven, with the cold sheet on the second set of runners. Bake for 30–35 minutes, until golden brown and shrinking away from the sides of the tin.

THREE- AND FOUR-OVEN AGA Slide the tin onto the grid shelf on the floor of the baking oven and bake for 30–35 minutes, until golden brown and shrinking away from the sides of the tin. If the cake is getting too brown, slide the cold shelf onto the second set of runners.

CONVENTIONAL OVEN Bake in a preheated oven (180°C/350°F/160°C Fan/Gas 4) for about 45 minutes.

Leave to cool in the tin.

Secret
- You can buy milk chocolate or dark chocolate chips in packets. I prefer to buy the dark ones as they have a stronger chocolate flavour.

SPICED FRUIT TRAYBAKE

This is quite a plain cake but has a lovely combination of mixed spice and dried fruit. It freezes well.

- Cuts into 16 pieces

>   225 g (8 oz) baking margarine, from the fridge
>   225 g (8 oz) caster sugar
>   300 g (10 oz) self-raising flour
>   2 tsp baking powder
>   4 eggs
>   4 tbsp milk
>   2 tsp mixed spice
>   75 g (3 oz) sultanas
>   50 g (2 oz) currants
>   50 g (2 oz) natural glacé cherries, rinsed, dried and cut into quarters

- Topping

>   40 g (1½ oz) flaked almonds

You will need a small Aga roasting tin (or traybake tin measuring 30 x 23 cm/12 x 9 in), lined with foil and greased.

Measure all the cake ingredients in a bowl and mix together until smooth. Pour into the prepared tin and sprinkle with the flaked almonds.

Two-oven Aga Slide the tin onto the grid shelf on the floor of the roasting oven with the cold sheet on the second set of runners. Bake for 25–30 minutes, until golden brown and shrinking away from the sides of the tin and springy to the touch.

Three- and four-oven Aga Slide the tin onto the lowest set of runners in the baking oven and bake for 25–30 minutes, until golden brown and shrinking away from the sides of the tin and springy to the touch. If the cake is getting too brown, slide the cold sheet onto the second set of runners.

Conventional oven Bake in a preheated oven (180°C/350°F/160°C Fan/Gas 4) for about 30 minutes.

Leave to cool in the tin.

Secret

- Natural glacé cherries are dark red. They are the same as the common glacé cherries but not bright red, which is a fake colouring. If you prefer the look of these, you can, of course, use them. Be sure to rinse the sticky syrup from the cherries and dry well, otherwise the cherries will sink to the bottom of the cake.

VANILLA TRAYBAKE

A classic vanilla sponge with no fancy flavours, just the true flavour of vanilla. It freezes well.

- Cuts into 16 pieces

  225 g (8 oz) baking margarine, from the fridge
  225 g (8 oz) caster sugar
  300 g (10 oz) self-raising flour
  2 tsp baking powder
  4 eggs
  4 tbsp milk
  2 tsp vanilla extract

- For topping

  About 3 tbsp demerara sugar

You will need a small Aga roasting tin (or traybake tin measuring 30 x 23 cm/12 x 9 in), lined with foil and greased.

Measure all the cake ingredients in a bowl and mix together until smooth. Pour into the prepared tin.

TWO-OVEN AGA Slide the tin onto the grid shelf on the floor of the roasting oven with the cold sheet on the second set of runners. Bake for 25–30 minutes, until golden brown and shrinking away from the sides of the tin and springy to the touch.

THREE- AND FOUR-OVEN AGA Slide the tin onto the lowest set of runners in the baking oven and bake for 25–30 minutes, until golden brown and shrinking away from the sides of the tin and springy to the touch. If the cake is getting too brown, slide the cold sheet onto the second set of runners.

CONVENTIONAL OVEN Bake in a preheated oven (180°C/350°F/160°C Fan/Gas 4) for about 30 minutes.

Leave to cool in the tin and then dust with icing sugar to serve.

Secret

- Buy vanilla extract and not vanilla essence. Extract is the real flavour taken from vanilla pods and essence is a manufactured flavour. If you have vanilla caster sugar, you can use this instead of the plain sugar.

ORANGE AND COCONUT TRAYBAKE

This is one of my favourite traybake recipes. It is a slightly unusual combination, but full of orange and coconut flavour. It freezes well un-iced.

- Cuts into 16 pieces

>   225 g (8 oz) baking margarine, from the fridge
>   225 g (8 oz) caster sugar
>   300 g (10 oz) self-raising flour
>   2 tsp baking powder
>   4 eggs
>   4 tbsp milk
>   75 g (3 oz) desiccated coconut
>   Grated rind of 2 oranges

- For the icing

>   225 g (8 oz) icing sugar
>   3 tbsp orange juice
>   About 25 g (1 oz) desiccated coconut

You will need a small Aga roasting tin (or traybake tin measuring 30 x 23 cm/12 x 9 in), lined with foil and greased.

Measure all the cake ingredients together in a bowl and mix together until smooth. Pour into the prepared tin.

TWO-OVEN AGA Slide the tin onto the grid shelf on the floor of the roasting oven with the cold sheet on the second set of runners. Bake for 25–30 minutes, until golden brown and shrinking away from the sides of the tin and springy to the touch.

THREE- AND FOUR-OVEN AGA Slide the tin onto the lowest set of runners in the baking oven and bake for 25–30 minutes, until golden brown and shrinking away from the sides of the tin and springy to the touch. If the cake is getting too brown, slide the cold sheet onto the second set of runners.

CONVENTIONAL OVEN Bake in a preheated oven (180°C/350°F/160°C Fan/Gas 4) for about 30 minutes.

Leave to cool in the tin.

To make the icing, sieve the icing sugar over a bowl, mix in the orange juice and beat until smooth. Spread evenly over the cake and sprinkle over the coconut.

Secret
- Desiccated coconut has a fine texture, therefore the cake will have texture to it. It can be found near the dried fruits in supermarkets.

Orange and coconut traybake (left) and Wholewheat apricot and almond traybake (right, see page 22)

WHOLEWHEAT APRICOT AND ALMOND TRAYBAKE

A classic traybake with added wholewheat flour to give a nutty healthy flavour. It freezes well. (See the photograph on page 21.)

- Cuts into 16 pieces

> 225 g (8 oz) baking margarine, from the fridge
> 225 g (8 oz) light muscovado sugar
> 225 g (8 oz) self-raising flour
> 50 g (2 oz) wholewheat plain flour
> 2 tsp baking powder
> 4 eggs
> 4 tbsp milk
> 2 tsp almond extract
> 50 g (2 oz) ground almonds
> 100 g (4 oz) dried apricots, snipped into small pieces

- Topping

> 40 g (1½ oz) flaked almonds

You will need a small Aga roasting tin (or traybake tin measuring 30 x 23 cm/12 x 9 in), lined with foil and greased.

Measure all the cake ingredients in a bowl and mix together until smooth. Pour into the prepared tin and sprinkle with the flaked almonds.

TWO-OVEN AGA Slide the tin onto the grid shelf on the floor of the roasting oven with the cold sheet on the second set of runners. Bake for 25–30 minutes, until golden brown and shrinking away from the sides of the tin and springy to the touch.

THREE- AND FOUR-OVEN AGA Slide the tin onto the lowest set of runners in the baking oven and bake for 25–30 minutes, until golden brown and shrinking away from the sides of the tin and springy to the touch. If the cake is getting too brown, slide the cold sheet onto the second set of runners.

CONVENTIONAL OVEN Bake in a preheated oven (180°C/350°F/160°C Fan/Gas 4) for about 30 minutes.

Leave to cool in the tin.

Secret

- All dried apricots in this book are the dried, ready-to-eat variety, not the ones that need soaking in liquid before using.

CHOCOLATE AND PECAN TRAYBAKE

This wonderful cake can be made with walnuts instead of pecans if preferred. It freezes well iced or un-iced.

- Cuts into 16 pieces

> 225 g (8 oz) baking margarine, from the fridge
> 225 g (8 oz) caster sugar
> 225 g (8 oz) self-raising flour
> 50 g (2 oz) cocoa powder
> 2 tsp baking powder
> 4 eggs
> 4 tbsp milk
> 75 g (3 oz) pecans, chopped

- For the icing

> 75 g (3 oz) butter, softened
> 225 g (8 oz) icing sugar, sifted
> 2 tbsp cocoa powder
> 1½ tbsp boiling water
> Pecans for decoration, sliced thinly

You will need a small Aga roasting tin (or traybake tin measuring 30 x 23 cm/12 x 9 in), lined with foil and greased.

Measure all the cake ingredients in a bowl and mix together until smooth. Pour into the prepared tin.

TWO-OVEN AGA Slide the tin onto the grid shelf on the floor of the roasting oven with the cold sheet on the second set of runners. Bake for 25–30 minutes, until golden brown and shrinking away from the sides of the tin and springy to the touch.

THREE- AND FOUR-OVEN AGA Slide the tin onto the lowest set of runners in the baking oven and bake for 25–30 minutes, until golden brown. If the cake is getting too brown, slide the cold sheet onto the second set of runners.

CONVENTIONAL OVEN Bake in a preheated oven (180°C/350°F/160°C Fan/Gas 4) for 35–40 minutes.

Leave to cool in the tin.

To make the icing, mix everything together, except the pecans, and beat until smooth. Spread evenly over the cold cake and set aside to become firm and then decorate with the sliced pecans.

Secret

- Measure the baking powder accurately. If you add too much, the cake will rise high and fall down again, leaving a dip in the centre of the cake.

MINCEMEAT AND ORANGE TRAYBAKE

Mincemeat cake is a huge favourite, especially at Christmas time. To make it extra special, serve warm with brandy butter. It freezes well.

- Cuts into 16 pieces

> 225 g (8 oz) baking margarine, from the fridge
> 225 g (8 oz) caster sugar
> 300 g (10 oz) self-raising flour
> 2 tsp baking powder
> 4 eggs
> 2 tbsp milk
> About half a 410 g jar of good mincemeat
> Finely grated rind of 1 large orange

- For the topping

> About 3 tbsp demerara sugar

You will need a small Aga roasting tin (or traybake tin measuring 30 x 23 cm/12 x 9 in), lined with foil and greased.

Measure all the cake ingredients together in a bowl and mix together until smooth. Pour into the prepared tin and sprinkle with the demerara sugar.

TWO-OVEN AGA Slide the tin onto the grid shelf on the floor of the roasting oven with the cold sheet on the second set of runners. Bake for 30–35 minutes, until golden brown and shrinking away from the sides of the tin and springy to the touch.

THREE- AND FOUR-OVEN AGA Slide the tin onto the lowest set of runners in the baking oven and bake for 30–35 minutes, until golden brown and shrinking away from the sides of the tin and springy to the touch. If the cake is getting too brown, slide the cold sheet onto the second set of runners.

CONVENTIONAL OVEN Bake in a preheated oven (180°C/350°F/160°C Fan/Gas 4) for about 40 minutes.

Leave to cool in the tin.

Secret

- Be sure to be accurate with the milk. If you add too much, the mixture will be too soft and the fruit will then sink to the bottom of the cake.

ESPRESSO COFFEE TRAYBAKE

Here is a deliciously simple coffee cake just as it is – no added flavours are needed. It freezes well un-iced.

- Cuts into 16 pieces

> 3 tbsp instant coffee
> 1 tbsp boiling water
> 225 g (8 oz) baking margarine, from the fridge
> 225 g (8 oz) caster sugar
> 300 g (10 oz) self-raising flour
> 2 tsp baking powder
> 4 eggs
> 4 tbsp milk

- For the icing

> 1 tbsp instant coffee
> ½ tbsp boiling water
> 75 g (3 oz) butter, softened
> 150 g (5 oz) icing sugar, sifted

You will need a small Aga roasting tin (or traybake tin measuring 30 x 23 cm/12 x 9 in), lined with foil and greased.

Measure the coffee into a mixing bowl and pour in the boiling water and mix to a smooth paste. Add the remaining cake ingredients and mix until smooth. Pour into the prepared tin.

TWO-OVEN AGA Slide the tin onto the grid shelf on the floor of the roasting oven with the cold sheet on the second set of runners. Bake for 25–30 minutes, until golden brown and shrinking away from the sides of the tin and springy to the touch.

THREE- AND FOUR-OVEN AGA Slide the tin onto the lowest set of runners in the baking oven and bake for 25–30 minutes, until golden brown and shrinking away from the sides of the tin and springy to the touch. If the cake is getting too brown, slide the cold sheet onto the second set of runners.

CONVENTIONAL OVEN Bake in a preheated oven (180°C/350°F/160°C Fan/Gas 4) for about 30 minutes.

Leave to cool in the tin.

To make the icing, measure the coffee into a bowl and mix with the boiling water to make a paste. Stir in the soft butter and icing sugar. Spread over the cold cake and run a fork over the icing to give a ridged effect.

Secret
- Taste the coffee mixture before baking. If you would like it stronger, add a little more coffee paste.

CLASSIC VICTORIA SANDWICH

A good Victoria sandwich is the perfect cake, looks impressive and will be loved by all. For variations, add the finely grated rind of two lemons, oranges or limes into the sponge mixture. It freezes well plain or filled.

- Cuts into 6–8 wedges

> 225 g (8 oz) butter, softened
> 225 g (8 oz) caster sugar
> 225 g (8 oz) self-raising flour
> 2 level tsp baking powder
> 4 eggs

- For the filling and topping

> 3 tbsp raspberry jam
> A little caster sugar

You will need two 20 cm (8 in)-diameter loose-bottomed sandwich tins, each greased and base lined with a disc of non-stick baking parchment.

Measure all the cake ingredients into a large bowl and mix together until smooth. Divide the mixture evenly between the prepared tins and level the tops.

TWO-OVEN AGA Slide the tins onto the grid shelf on the floor of the roasting oven, with the cold sheet on the second set of runners. Bake for about 20 minutes, until golden brown and shrinking away from the sides of the tins and springy to the touch.

THREE- AND FOUR-OVEN AGA Slide the tins onto the grid shelf on the floor of the baking oven and bake for 20–25 minutes, until golden brown and shrinking away from the sides of the tins and springy to the touch. If the cakes are getting too brown, slide the cold sheet onto the second set of runners.

CONVENTIONAL OVEN Bake in a preheated oven (180°C/350°F/160°C Fan/Gas 4) for 20–25 minutes, until well risen.

Leave to cool in the tins. Turn out and remove the baking parchment and turn one cake upside down. Spread with the jam and sit the other cake the right way up on top. Sprinkle the top with caster sugar and serve in slices.

Secrets
- If using baking margarine, use it straight from the fridge.

- Do not buy a spread as this has too much water in it and will make a flat cake.

LEMON DRIZZLE SANDWICH CAKE

My wonderful friend Mary Berry invented this recipe over 40 years ago and now it is one of the most popular cakes to make – lemon sponge with a crunchy lemon topping. It freezes well iced or un-iced.

- Cuts into 6–8 wedges

>   225 g (8 oz) butter or margarine, softened
>   225 g (8 oz) caster sugar
>   225 g (8 oz) self-raising flour
>   2 level tsp baking powder
>   4 eggs
>   Finely grated rind of 2 lemons

- For the filling and topping

>   About 2 tbsp lemon juice
>   175 g (6 oz) granulated sugar
>   3 good tbsp lemon curd

You will need two 20 cm (8 in)-diameter loose-bottomed sandwich tins, each greased and base lined with a disc of non-stick baking parchment.

Measure all the cake ingredients into a large bowl and mix together until smooth. Divide the mixture evenly between the prepared tins and level the tops.

TWO-OVEN AGA Slide the tins onto the grid shelf on the floor of the roasting oven, with the cold sheet on the second set of runners. Bake for about 20 minutes, until well risen and golden brown.

THREE- AND FOUR-OVEN AGA Slide the tins onto the grid shelf on the floor of the baking oven and bake for 20–25 minutes, until well risen and golden brown. If the cakes are getting too brown, slide the cold sheet onto the second set of runners.

CONVENTIONAL OVEN Bake in a preheated oven (180°C/350°F/160°C Fan/Gas 4) for 20–25 minutes, until well risen.

Leave to cool in the tins for a few moments.

Meanwhile, for the topping, mix together the lemon juice and sugar in a bowl. Turn one cake out from its tin and remove the baking parchment. Pour the lemon and sugar over the warm cake and set aside until firm. Once the other cake is cold, remove it from its tin, peel off the baking parchment and turn the cake upside down and sit on a plate. Spread with the lemon curd and sit the other cake on top.

Secret

- It is important to pour the sugar topping mixture on the warm cake so the lemon juice soaks into the sponge – if the cake is cold it will not soak into the cake.

GOLDEN SYRUP CAKE

This is a plain, simple cake but full of flavour – it just tastes of golden syrup! There is no need to ice it, just serve as is. It freezes well.

- Cuts into 6 wedges

> 100 g (4 oz) caster sugar
> 100 g (4 oz) baking margarine, from the fridge
> 175 g (6 oz) self-raising flour
> 1 tsp baking powder
> 2 eggs
> 100 g (4 oz) golden syrup

You will need a 20 cm (8 in)-diameter sandwich tin, greased and base lined with a disc of non-stick baking parchment.

Measure all the ingredients into a bowl and beat with a wooden spoon until smooth. Spoon into the prepared tin and level the top.

TWO-OVEN AGA Slide the tin onto the grid shelf on the floor of the roasting oven with the cold sheet on the second set of runners, Bake for 25–30 minutes, until golden brown, shrinking away from the sides of the tin and springy to the touch.

THREE- AND FOUR-OVEN AGA Slide the tin onto the grid shelf on the floor of the baking oven and bake for about 30 minutes, until well risen and golden brown, shrinking away from the sides of the tin and springy to the touch. If the cake is getting too brown, slide the cold sheet onto the second set of runners.

CONVENTIONAL OVEN Bake in a preheated oven (180°C/350°F/160°C Fan/Gas 4) for 30–35 minutes.

Leave to cool in the tin.

Secret
- The easiest way to measure golden syrup is to measure it on top of the sugar and then it does not stick to the scale pan. Weigh the sugar into the scale pan and then pour the syrup on top of the sugar until the combined weight is reached. The syrup sticks to the sugar and they both slide easily from the scale pan. Don't be tempted to add too much golden syrup otherwise the cake will be flat and will not rise.

STRAWBERRY SWISS ROLL

This classic tea time cake is best eaten very fresh as fatless sponges do not keep for long. Once made, keep it in the fridge. Vary the jam as you wish, and make the Swiss roll extra special by adding a few chopped fresh strawberries into the cream. This cake also doubles up as a dessert. It freezes well filled with cream and jam, not fresh strawberries. Once defrosted, serve fresh strawberries alongside.

- Cuts into 8 generous slices

> 4 eggs
> 100 g (4 oz) caster sugar, plus extra for sprinkling (optional)
> 100 g (4 oz) self-raising flour

- For the filling

> About 4 tbsp strawberry jam
> 300 ml (10 fl oz) double cream, whipped
> 75 g (3 oz) fresh strawberries, cut into quarters

You will need a Swiss roll tin measuring 33 x 23 cm (13 x 9 in). Cut a rectangle of non-stick baking parchment just larger than the base and sides of the tin. Grease the tin and then line with the baking parchment, pushing it neatly into the corners to fit.

Whisk the eggs and sugar, preferably using an electric hand whisk or tabletop electric mixer, until the mixture is light and frothy and has increased in volume. When the whisk is lifted out of the bowl, the mixture falling off it should leave a trail. Sift the flour into the mixture, carefully folding in at the same time using a metal spoon. Turn the mixture into the prepared tin, spreading it gently into the corners.

TWO-, THREE- AND FOUR-OVEN AGA Slide the tin onto the grid shelf on the floor of the roasting oven. Bake for about 8 minutes, until golden brown and shrinking away from the sides of the tin. Watch carefully as it can get too dark.

CONVENTIONAL OVEN Bake in a preheated oven (200°C/400°F/180°C Fan/Gas 6) for about 10 minutes. Watch the cake very carefully as it easy to over-bake it.

Place a piece of non-stick baking parchment a little bigger than the size of the tin onto a work surface and sprinkle it with caster sugar. While still warm, invert the cake onto the sugared paper. Quickly loosen the baking parchment on the bottom of the cake and peel it away. Trim the edges of the sponge with a sharp knife and make a score mark 2 cm (¾ in) in from one shorter edge, being careful not to cut right through. Roll up the cake firmly with the baking parchment inside. Work from the shorter, cut end, tucking in the scored piece of sponge tightly to make a roll. Leave to cool.

Once stone cold, carefully unroll the cake, remove the baking parchment and spread with the jam. Whip the cream until just stiff and fold in the strawberries. Spread the cream mixture over the jam. Re-roll the cake tightly and in the same way you rolled it to begin with, using the baking parchment to guide you. Sprinkle with a little more caster sugar, if you want. Keep in the fridge until needed, but eat as fresh as possible.

Secrets

- It is important to get as much air into the egg and sugar mixture as possible, so whisk with a large whisk.
- To get extra volume, warm the sugar in the simmering or plate warming oven of the Aga.

Chocolate cakes

Everyone loves chocolate and this wouldn't be a proper cake book without it! These sumptuous delights are equally good served as teatime cakes and some are good as dinner-party desserts too.

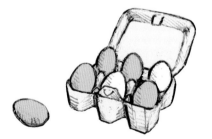

THE ULTIMATE CHOCOLATE CAKE

This is not only delicious, it looks very impressive too – cut into four layers, it stands tall and proud! It freezes well un-iced.

- Cuts into 8–10 wedges

- For the icing and filling

> 150 g (5 oz) dark chocolate, broken into small pieces
> 150 ml (¼ pint) pouring double cream
> 50 g (2 oz) white chocolate chips or white chocolate buttons

- For the cake

> 50 g (2 oz) cocoa powder
> 6 tbsp boiling water
> 225 g (8 oz) baking margarine, softened
> 225 g (8 oz) caster sugar
> 225 g (8 oz) self-raising flour
> 2 tsp baking powder
> 4 eggs

You will need two 20 cm (8 in)-diameter loose-bottomed sandwich tins, each greased and base lined with a disc of non-stick baking parchment.

For the icing and filling, measure the dark chocolate and cream into a heatproof bowl and put on the back of the Aga, stirring occasionally until melted. (For a conventional oven, melt the chocolate and cream in a bowl standing over a saucepan of hot water until melted.) Once melted, set aside and allow to become cold and slightly thicker (ready for icing).

For the cake, measure the cocoa powder into a mixing bowl and blend with the boiling water until well mixed. Add the remaining cake ingredients and mix until smooth and combined. Divide the cake mixture between the prepared tins.

TWO-OVEN AGA Slide the tins onto the grid shelf on the floor of the roasting oven with the cold sheet on the second set of runners. Bake for 20–25 minutes, until well risen and shrinking away from the sides of the tins and springy to the touch.

THREE- AND FOUR-OVEN AGA Slide the tins onto the grid shelf on the floor of the baking oven and bake for 20–25 minutes, until shrinking away from the sides of the tins and springy to the touch. If the cakes are getting too brown, slide the cold sheet onto the second set of runners above for the last few minutes.

CONVENTIONAL OVEN Bake in a preheated oven (180°C/350°F/160°C Fan/Gas 4) for about 25 minutes.

Remove the cakes from the tins and allow to cool completely. Once cold, slice each cake in half horizontally using a bread knife. Sit one cake base on a plate and spread with a quarter of the dark chocolate icing. Continue layering up the cake with the icing, finishing with

one of the tops of the cakes. Spread the top evenly with the dark chocolate and then arrange the chocolate chips in even parallel lines across the top. Transfer the whole cake to the simmering oven for 3 minutes (or the turned-off warm conventional oven), just enough time for the chips to melt slightly. Using the end of a teaspoon, drag through the lines of the melted chocolate drops. Set aside to firm up.

Secrets

- After melting the chocolate, set it aside to cool in the kitchen away from the Aga – do not put in the fridge otherwise the icing becomes dull and loses its lovely sheen. The icing needs to thicken slightly so it can be spooned rather than poured, otherwise it will pour off the cake.

- Use a bread knife to cut through the cakes using a sawing action.

- To create feathering, drag the teaspoon in alternating directions through the chocolate.

FOOLPROOF CHOCOLATE CAKE WITH FUDGE ICING

This cake is very simple to make using the all-in-one method – I promise it will be perfect! It freezes well, too.

- Cuts into 6–8 wedges

  100 g (4 oz) self-raising flour
  25 g (1 oz) cocoa powder
  1 tsp baking powder
  100 g (4 oz) caster sugar
  6 tbsp sunflower oil
  3 tbsp milk
  2 eggs

- For the fudge icing

  25 g (1 oz) margarine
  1 tbsp cocoa powder
  About 1 tbsp milk
  100 g (4 oz) icing sugar, sifted,
    plus extra for dusting
  A little warmed strawberry jam

You will need a 20 cm (8 in)-diameter loose-bottomed sandwich cake tin, greased and base lined with a disc of baking parchment.

Measure the flour, cocoa powder, baking powder and sugar into a mixing bowl. Pour the oil, milk and eggs into a jug and beat together with a fork. Pour into the flour mixture and beat with a wooden spoon or electric hand whisk until smooth. Spoon into the prepared tin and level the top.

TWO-OVEN AGA Slide the tin onto the grid shelf on the floor of the roasting oven. Bake for 20–25 minutes, until risen and shrinking away from the sides of the tin.

THREE- AND FOUR-OVEN AGA Slide the tin onto the grid shelf on the floor of the baking oven and bake for about 25 minutes, until lightly golden brown, well risen and shrinking away from the sides of the tin. If the cake is getting too brown, slide the cold sheet onto the second set of runners.

CONVENTIONAL OVEN Bake in a preheated oven (180°C/350°F/160°C Fan/Gas 4) for about 30 minutes.

Leave to cool in the tin, then turn out and remove the baking parchment.

To make the fudge icing, melt the margarine in a small pan, add the cocoa powder and cook for a minute. Remove from the heat and stir in the milk and icing sugar. Beat well with a wooden spoon until smooth, then set aside to thicken for about 10 minutes, until it has a spreading consistency. Spread the top of the cake with the warmed strawberry jam and then spread the fudge icing over the top and sides and dust with icing sugar to serve.

Secrets
- Warming the jam makes it easier to spread over the cake.
- Covering the top of the cake with jam prevents the crumbs from the cake from mixing in with the icing and also keeps the cake moist.

BLACK FOREST SWISS ROLL

This is such an easy cake to make and it only takes 8 minutes to bake. To make this cake extra special, melt 100 g (4 oz) dark chocolate and spread over the cold cake before rolling. Once made, keep in the fridge. It freezes well filled and rolled.

- Cuts into 8 generous slices

    4 eggs
    100 g (4 oz) caster sugar, plus
        extra for sprinkling (optional)
    75 g (3 oz) self-raising flour
    25 g (1 oz) cocoa powder

- For the filling

    About 4 tbsp black cherry jam
    300 ml (10 fl oz) double cream,
        whipped

You will need a Swiss roll tin measuring 33 x 23 cm (13 x 9 in). Cut a rectangle of non-stick baking parchment just larger than the base and sides of the tin. Grease the tin and then line with the baking parchment, pushing it neatly into the corners to fit.

Whisk the eggs and sugar, preferably using an electric hand whisk or tabletop electric mixer, until the mixture is light and frothy and has increased in volume. When the whisk is lifted out of the bowl, the mixture falling off it should leave a trail. Sift the flour into the mixture, carefully folding in at the same time using a metal spoon. Turn the mixture into the prepared tin, spreading it gently into the corners.

TWO-, THREE- AND FOUR-OVEN AGA Slide the tin onto the grid shelf on the floor of the roasting oven. Bake for about 8 minutes, until golden brown and shrinking away from the sides of the tin. Watch carefully as it can get too dark.

CONVENTIONAL OVEN Bake in a preheated oven (200°C/400°F/180°C Fan/Gas 6) for about 10 minutes. Watch the cake very carefully as it easy to over-bake it.

Place a piece of non-stick baking parchment a little bigger than the size of the tin onto a work surface and sprinkle it with caster sugar. While still warm, invert the cake onto the sugared paper. Quickly loosen the baking parchment on the bottom of the cake and peel it away. Trim the edges of the sponge with a sharp knife and make a score mark 2 cm (¾ in) in from one shorter edge, being careful not to cut right through. Roll up the cake firmly with the baking parchment inside. Work from the shorter, cut end, tucking in the scored piece of sponge tightly to make a roll. Leave to cool.

Once stone cold, carefully unroll the cake, remove the baking parchment and spread with the jam and whipped cream. Re-roll the cake tightly and in the same way you rolled it to begin with, using the baking parchment to guide you. Sprinkle with a little more caster sugar, if you want.

Keep in the fridge until needed, but eat as fresh as possible.

Secret

- I have tested this recipe in the Aga small roasting tin but it really made the cake too thick to roll, so you do need a Swiss roll tin or classic traybake tin.

CHOCOLATE FRUIT TIFFIN

This is so quick to make and reminiscent of my childhood; it is quite an old-fashioned recipe. It is very rich, so only serve small pieces. It freezes well.

- Cuts into 32 pieces

> 200 g (7 oz) dark chocolate
> 350 g (12 oz) digestive biscuits
> 2 good tbsp golden syrup
> 175 g (6 oz) baking margarine, from the fridge
> 225 g (8 oz) mixed dried fruit, such as sultanas, raisins and snipped apricots
> 50 g (2 oz) glacé cherries, rinsed, dried and cut into small pieces

You will need a small Aga roasting tin (or a small roasting tin measuring 30 x 23 cm/ 12 x 9 in). Cut a rectangle of non-stick baking parchment just larger than the base and sides of the tin. Grease the tin and then line with the baking parchment, pushing it neatly into the corners to fit.

Break the chocolate into a bowl and sit on the back of the Aga to melt. (For a conventional oven, put the chocolate into a bowl and heat gently over a pan of simmering water, stirring until melted.)

Crush the digestive biscuits in a poly bag with a rolling pin until small, fine pieces. Melt the golden syrup and margarine in a pan on the simmering plate (or on the hob set to a low heat), then add the dried fruits and crushed biscuits and mix well.

Tip into the prepared tin, level out and leave to set in the fridge. Once set, pour the melted chocolate over the biscuit base and leave to set, once again, and become hard in the fridge.

When completely cold, cut into eight slices across the long side and four pieces across the short side and store in the fridge.

Secrets
- Stir the chocolate occasionally when melting as this will help it to melt quicker.

- If you are short of time, you can also melt the chocolate in the simmering oven, but watch carefully so it does not get too hot.

Chocolate fruit tiffin (left) and The very best chocolate brownies (right, see page 40)

THE VERY BEST CHOCOLATE BROWNIES

This is a recipe I have been making for years and it is loved by all. Don't worry if the brownie dips in the middle, it is part of its charm – a brownie is dense and gooey in the middle, not light and fluffy like other cakes. They freeze well. (See the photograph on page 39.)

- Cuts into 20 brownies

> 350 g (12 oz) dark chocolate
> 225 g (8 oz) butter, softened
> 4 eggs
> 225 g (8 oz) caster sugar
> 75 g (3 oz) self-raising flour

You will need a small Aga roasting tin (or roasting tin measuring about 30 x 23 cm/ 12 x 9 in), lined with foil and greased.

Measure the chocolate and butter into a bowl and sit on the back of the Aga until melted. (For a conventional oven, put the chocolate and butter into a bowl and heat gently over a pan of simmering water, stirring until melted.)

Using a wooden spoon, beat the eggs and sugar in a large bowl until combined. Pour in the melted chocolate and butter and stir. Stir in the flour and beat until smooth and then pour into the prepared tin.

TWO-OVEN AGA Slide the tin onto the grid shelf on the floor of the roasting oven with the cold sheet on the second set of runners. Bake for about 20 minutes, until fairly firm. Transfer the now hot cold sheet to the simmering oven, slide the tin on top and continue to bake for a further 20 minutes, until firm and a light crust has formed on top.

THREE- AND FOUR-OVEN AGA Slide the tin onto the grid shelf on the floor of the baking oven and bake for about 25 minutes. After this time, slide the cold sheet onto the second set of runners and continue to cook for a further 10 minutes, until firm and a light crust has formed on top.

CONVENTIONAL OVEN Bake in a preheated oven (190°C/375°F/170°C Fan/Gas 5) for 40–45 minutes.

Leave to cool in the tin.

Secret

- A dip in the middle of the cake means it is nice and gooey, just how a brownie should be. Don't be tempted to overcook otherwise it will dry out; it is best to be softer rather than dry.

MARBLE TRAYBAKE

This cake looks so attractive as the marble effect looks stunning – and it is so tasty too. It freezes well un-iced.

- Cuts into 16 pieces

  200 g (8 oz) baking margarine, from the fridge
  200 g (8 oz) caster sugar
  300 g (10 oz) self-raising flour
  2 tsp baking powder
  4 eggs
  2 tbsp milk

  ½ tsp vanilla extract
  1½ tbsp cocoa powder
  2 tbsp hot water

- For the icing

  25 g (1 oz) margarine
  1 tbsp cocoa powder
  4 tbsp milk
  200 g (8 oz) icing sugar, sifted

You will need a small Aga roasting tin (or traybake tin measuring 30 x 23 cm/12 x 9 in), lined with foil and greased.

Measure the margarine, sugar, flour, baking powder, eggs, milk and vanilla extract into a large mixing bowl and beat well for about 2 minutes, until well blended. Spoon half of the mixture into another bowl and set aside.

In a small bowl, mix together the cocoa powder and hot water until smooth. Allow to cool slightly, then add to one of the bowls of cake mixture, mixing well until evenly blended.

Spoon the vanilla and chocolate mixture in alternate spoonfuls in the tin and level the top. Using the handle of a teaspoon, drag in a figure of eight the chocolate and vanilla mixtures across the tin to give a marble effect.

TWO-OVEN AGA Slide the tin onto the grid shelf on the floor of the roasting oven with the cold sheet on the second set of runners. Bake for 25–30 minutes, until shrinking away from the sides of the tin and springy to the touch.

THREE- AND FOUR-OVEN AGA Slide the tin onto the lowest set of runners in the baking oven and bake for about 20 minutes, until shrinking away from the sides of the tin and springy to the touch. If the cake is getting too brown, slide the cold sheet onto the second set of runners.

CONVENTIONAL OVEN Bake in a preheated oven (180°C/350°F/160°C Fan/Gas 4) for about 30 minutes.

Leave to cool in the tin.

For the icing, melt the margarine in a small pan, add the cocoa powder and stir to blend. Remove from the heat, stir in the milk and icing sugar, and mix thoroughly. Spread over the cold cake and, using a palette knife, swirl 'S' shapes across the icing to give a pretty effect.

Secret
- It is important to swirl the two mixtures together with the handle of a teaspoon otherwise the cake will just appear to be two-tone vanilla and chocolate and not marbled.

WHITE CHOCOLATE MAPLE CAKE

I adore this cake and it has an unusual cooking method and flavour – similar to a yoghurt cake, the white chocolate adds a lovely creamy flavour. It freezes well un-iced.

- Cuts into 6–8 wedges

> 100 g (4 oz) good quality white chocolate
> 175 g (6 oz) butter, softened
> 100 g (4 oz) caster sugar
> 3 eggs
> 300 g (10 oz) self-raising flour
> I tsp baking powder
> 175 g (6 oz) maple syrup
> 150 ml (¼ pint) milk

- For the filling and icing

> I x 250 g tub full-fat mascarpone cheese
> 3 tbsp maple syrup
> I heaped tbsp icing sugar
> Snowflake chocolate bar for decoration (optional)

You will need two 20 cm (8 in)-diameter loose-bottomed sandwich tins, each greased and base lined with a disc of non-stick baking parchment.

Measure the white chocolate into a bowl and sit on the back of the Aga to melt, stirring occasionally. (For a conventional oven, put the white chocolate into a bowl and heat gently over a pan of simmering water, stirring until melted.) Once melted, set aside to cool a little.

Measure the butter and sugar into a bowl and beat with a wooden spoon until creamy and fluffy. Beat in the eggs (do not worry, it will look curdled at this stage – keep going!). Then beat in the flour, baking powder and maple syrup and stir until combined. Gradually add the milk, beating as you add it until combined. Pour in the melted chocolate and stir until smooth. Spoon into the prepared tins and level the tops.

TWO-OVEN AGA Slide the tins onto the grid shelf on the floor of the roasting oven with the cold sheet on the second set of runners. Bake for about 30 minutes, until lightly golden brown, well risen and shrinking away from the sides of the tins.

THREE- AND FOUR-OVEN AGA Slide the tins onto the grid shelf on the floor of the baking oven and bake for about 35 minutes, until lightly golden brown, well risen and shrinking away from the sides of the tins. If the cakes are getting too brown, slide the cold sheet onto the second set of runners.

CONVENTIONAL OVEN Bake in a preheated oven (180°C/350°F/160°C Fan/Gas 4) for about 30 minutes.

Leave to cool in the tin, then turn out and remove the baking parchment.

To make the icing, mix together the mascarpone, maple syrup and icing sugar until smooth. Turn one cake upside down on a plate and spread with half the icing. Top with the other cake and spread the remaining icing on top. Crumble the chocolate bar and sprinkle over the top, if using.

Secret
- Use a good quality white chocolate and heat it gently on the back of the Aga. You may need to sit the bowl on a tea towel if it starts becoming hot – do not allow it to get too hot otherwise the chocolate will split and become oily.

CHOCOLATE AND FIG FRUIT LOAF

This cake has a lovely combination of figs and chocolate. The chocolate sponge is not too sweet as the figs are very sweet, compensating for the bitterness of the chocolate. Sometimes dried figs have a little stalk at the top of the fig; if you find one, snip it out with scissors and discard. The loaf freezes well un-iced.

- Makes 1 loaf that cuts into about 10 slices

      50 g (2 oz) cocoa powder
      6 tbsp boiling water
      100 g (4 oz) baking margarine, from the fridge
      175 g (6 oz) caster sugar
      100 g (4 oz) self-raising flour
      2 eggs, beaten
      2 tbsp milk
      150 g (5 oz) dried figs (about 8), cut into small pieces
      150 g (5 oz) sultanas

- To decorate

      Icing sugar

You will need a 450 g (1 lb) loaf tin, greased and lined with non-stick baking parchment.

Measure the cocoa powder into a large mixing bowl and pour over the water and mix to a smooth paste. Add the remaining ingredients into the bowl. Mix well until smooth and spoon into the prepared loaf tin, levelling the top.

TWO-OVEN AGA Slide the loaf tins onto the grid shelf on the floor of the roasting oven with the cold sheet on the second set of runners. Bake for about 30 minutes, until dark brown and the top forms a crust. Transfer the now hot cold sheet to the simmering oven, put the loaf on top and bake for a further hour, until set and cooked through. The cake is cooked when a skewer comes out clean when inserted into the centre of the cake.

THREE- AND FOUR-OVEN AGA Slide the loaf tins onto the grid shelf on the floor of the baking oven and bake for 50–60 minutes, until well risen and cooked through. If the cake is getting too brown, slide the cold sheet onto the second set of runners.

CONVENTIONAL OVEN Bake in a preheated oven (180°C/350°F/160°C Fan/Gas 4) for about 1¼ hours.

Leave to cool in the tin. Then score around the edge of the tin, remove the cake and the baking parchment. Dust with icing sugar and serve.

Secret
- The easiest way to line a loaf tin is to cut one piece of baking parchment to fit across the wide side of the tin from edge to edge. Do not worry about lining the ends of the tin, the cake will come out easily.

DIDDY CHOCOLATE CHIP MUFFINS

These are adorable, so easy to make and so cute too. For a naughty start to the day, these are lovely as a breakfast muffin as they are diddy and not too big at breakfast time. They freeze well.

- Makes 30 muffins

      25 g (1 oz) cocoa powder
      100 g (4 oz) self-raising flour
      75 g (3 oz) caster sugar
      1 rounded tsp baking powder
      1 egg
      50 g (2 oz) butter, melted
      150 ml (¼ pint) milk
      50 g (2 oz) dark chocolate chips

- To serve

      Icing sugar, for dusting

You will need three 12-hole mini muffin tins, greased or lined with paper cases.

Mix together the cocoa powder, flour, sugar and baking powder in a bowl. In a separate bowl mix together the egg, melted butter and milk with a fork until blended. Pour the liquid onto the flour mixture and mix with a wooden spoon until smooth. Stir in the chocolate chips and spoon into the mini muffin cases.

TWO-OVEN AGA Slide the tins onto the grid shelf on the floor of the roasting oven with the cold sheet on the second set of runners. Bake for about 12 minutes, until well risen and firm to the touch.

THREE- AND FOUR-OVEN AGA Slide the tins onto the grid shelf on the floor of the baking oven and bake for about 12 minutes, until well risen and firm to the touch.

CONVENTIONAL OVEN Bake in a preheated oven (200°C/400°F/180°C Fan/Gas 6) for 20–25 minutes.

Serve dusted with icing sugar.

Secrets
- If you like, replace the chocolate chips with the same quantity of sultanas, snipped dried apricots or fresh raspberries.

- This quantity also makes 12 full-size muffins.

DOUBLE CHOCOLATE CHOCOLATE CAKE

This is a posh chocolate cake and looks absolutely stunning. The contrast of the dark cake and white icing is very attractive. It freezes well un-iced.

- Cuts into 6–8 wedges

    225 g (8 oz) butter, softened
    225 g (8 oz) caster sugar
    100 g (4 oz) self-raising flour
    25 g (1 oz) cocoa powder
    1 tsp baking powder
    4 eggs
    75 g (3 oz) ground almonds

- For the white chocolate icing

    225 g (8 oz) white chocolate
    75 g (3 oz) butter, cubed
    White and Dark Chocolate curls,
      to decorate (see page 51)

You will need a deep, 23 cm (9 in)-diameter loose-bottomed cake tin or springform tin, greased and base lined with a disc of non-stick baking parchment.

Measure all the cake ingredients into a mixing bowl and beat with a wooden spoon or electric hand whisk until smooth. Spoon into the prepared tin and level the top.

TWO-OVEN AGA Slide the tin onto the grid shelf on the floor of the roasting oven with the cold sheet on the second set of runners. Bake for about 35 minutes, until risen and shrinking away from the sides of the tin.

THREE- AND FOUR-OVEN AGA Slide the tin onto the grid shelf on the floor of the baking oven and bake for about 30 minutes, until well risen and shrinking away from the sides of the tin. You may need to slide the cold sheet onto the second set of runners if the cake is getting too brown, so watch carefully.

CONVENTIONAL OVEN Bake in a preheated oven (180°C/350°F/160°C Fan/Gas 4) for about 40 minutes.

Run a palette knife around the sides of the tin and set aside to cool. Remove from the tin and discard the baking parchment.

To make the icing, break the chocolate into a bowl. Add the butter and sit on the back of the Aga until melted, stirring occasionally. (For a conventional oven, put the chocolate into a bowl and heat gently over a pan of simmering water, stirring until melted.) Set aside to cool and to thicken (do not put in the fridge). Using a palette knife, spread the top and sides of the cold cake with the white icing, making sure the icing is flat and smooth over the cake. Sprinkle with chocolate curls.

Transfer to the fridge until the icing is set.

Secret
- If you are worried about making chocolate curls, you can serve the cake plain, or dust with cocoa powder.

MINI-CHOCOLATE ECLAIRS

I think of chocolate éclairs as a posh tea time treat. It is very important to measure accurately. I have given you a choice of two easy toppings – chocolate or toffee. They freeze well filled but un-iced.

- Makes 28 mini éclairs

- For the choux pastry

    50 g (2 oz) butter
    150 ml (¼ pint) water
    60 g (2½ oz) flour
      (see secret, below)
    2 eggs, beaten

- For the filling

    300 ml (½ pint) whipping
      cream, whipped

- For the chocolate ganache icing

    50 g (2 oz) dark chocolate
    3 tbsp double cream

You will need a baking sheet, greased, and a piping bag and 1 cm (½ in) plain nozzle.

Measure the butter into a pan, pour in the water and gently bring to the boil on the simmering plate (or on the hob set to a low heat) until the butter has melted (do not boil for longer than 5 seconds otherwise the water will evaporate). Remove from the heat, quickly add the flour all at once and beat with a wooden spoon until it forms a ball around the spoon.

Gradually beat in the eggs, a little at a time, to give a smooth glossy paste. Fit the piping bag with the nozzle and spoon the mixture into the bag. Pipe 24 x 5 cm (2 in) lengths, keeping them fairly well spaced to give them room to spread a little.

Two-, three- and four-oven Aga Slide the baking sheet onto the lowest set of runners in the roasting oven and bake for about 15 minutes, until light golden brown and well risen.

Conventional oven Bake in a preheated oven (220°C/425°F/200°C Fan/Gas 7) for about 15 minutes. Don't turn off the oven yet.

Set aside to cool a little. Once cool enough to handle, snip with a pair of scissors along the length of the éclair to allow the steam to escape (this prevents the éclairs from becoming soggy). Transfer the baking sheet to the simmering oven for about 10 minutes to completely dry out inside. (If baked in a conventional oven, return the éclairs to the cooled oven for about 10 minutes to dry out.)

Spoon the whipped cream into the cleaned piping bag and nozzle and pipe the cream into the cold éclairs, along the slit that you made earlier. You can also spoon the cream into the centre if you find this easier than piping.

For the icing, break the chocolate into a bowl and pour over the cream. Sit on the back of the Aga, stirring occasionally until melted. (For a conventional oven, put the chocolate and cream into a bowl and heat gently over a pan of simmering water, stirring until melted.) Using a teaspoon, spread each éclair with the melted icing or, if easier, dip the éclair into the icing. Set aside for the icing to set.

Secrets
- To prevent choux pastry from curdling, add the flour quickly in one go and gradually

add the beaten eggs and beat hard between each addition — you need to have strong arm muscles to make éclairs!

- I have made choux pastry with both plain flour and self-raising flour and I could not tell the difference — both were very successful.

Variation
- Toffee topping

> **6 soft toffees**
> **2 tbsp double cream**

Gently melt the toffees and cream together in a pan on the simmering plate (or on the hob set to a low heat). Once melted, spoon over the éclairs using a teaspoon. You have to put the icing on immediately otherwise the toffee icing will set too hard to spread.

INDULGENT CHOCOLATE AND HAZELNUT TRUFFLES

You must use 70% cocoa solid chocolate for this recipe otherwise the truffles won't set. Serve straight from the fridge but hide them at the back until needed, otherwise they will be pinched every time the fridge door is opened! They are good to serve as a special treat with coffee or after a meal. Not suitable for freezing.

- Makes about 60 truffles

> 300 g (10 oz) dark chocolate, 70% cocoa solid
> 300 ml (½ pint) double cream
> 2 tbsp Cointreau, Grand Marnier, Brandy or Rum
> 50 g (2 oz) roasted chopped hazelnuts

- To serve

> Cocoa powder or icing sugar, for dusting (optional)

You will need an 18 cm (7 in)-square tin, lined with cling film, and petit four cases to serve the truffles.

Break the chocolate into chunks. Measure the cream into a pan and bring to the boil on the boiling plate. Remove from the heat, add the chocolate pieces and Cointreau (or whatever alternative you choose) and stir until the chocolate has dissolved in the hot cream.

Pour into the lined tin, set aside to cool and then place in the fridge overnight.

Cut the set chocolate mixture into neat 2 cm (¾ in) cubes. Roll into a ball using your hands, roll in the chopped hazelnuts and then sit in a petit four case. Keep in the fridge for up to ten days.

Just before serving, dust with a little cocoa powder or icing sugar, if liked.

Secret

- If you are not keen on nuts, just roll the balls in cocoa powder or icing sugar.

IDEAS FOR CHOCOLATE CAKE DECORATION

Often the simplest decoration is the most attractive. For children's cakes, use a variety of different sweets as decoration, such as:

> Maltesers
> Chocolate buttons
> Matchmaker chocolates
> Flake and Snowflake

Get the decoration ready before icing the cake and then decorate immediately as most icings 'set'. Arranging a decoration once the icing has set will spoil the effect of the cake. I find Bournville chocolate the easiest to use, you can buy it practically everywhere and it is pretty foolproof to use.

CHOCOLATE CURLS For simple chocolate curls, use a potato peeler along the flat underside of a bar of chocolate. The bar of chocolate should be at room temperature, if too cold the chocolate will flake and not curl.

For really professional chocolate curls (chocolate caraque), melt plain or white chocolate and pour a thin layer onto a marble slab or granite worksurface. Spread to a thin layer with a palette knife and leave to set and go cloudy for a few moments. Using a sharp, long-bladed knife, hold the knife at an angle and shave the chocolate off the surface to form curls. I find it easiest to keep my fingers on the blade and press from the blade so it stays in contact with the surface.

CHOCOLATE LEAVES Using a small paintbrush, spread melted chocolate evenly onto the surface of a clean, dry leaf. Leave to set and gently peel the leaf off the chocolate – not the chocolate from the leaf otherwise it may split.

CHOCOLATE SHAPES Chocolate shapes can look very pretty and impressive and are easiest to make with a piping bag. Just use melted chocolate and pipe different shapes onto non-stick baking parchment and leave to set. For the perfect shape, trace different outlines onto the baking parchment and pipe over the lines.

FEATHERING Feathering can look stunning on a cake. It looks impressive, but is very simple to do. To get the effect, you need to use dark and white chocolate. Ice the cake with the icing and, using the contrasting chocolate, pipe or drizzle evenly spaced parallel lines. Before the icing sets, drag the handle of a teaspoon or skewer across the lines in alternating directions. To give a spider's web effect, pipe or drizzle the contrasting colour in circles and drag from the centre in alternating directions.

Baking with kids

Childhood memories should be scattered with cooking at home, just as mine are. Many of my friends want recipes they can make with their children, so they need to be quick and easy to make and fun to do. All the recipes in this chapter are just that, so that children don't have to wait too long to taste their creations!

CHOCOLATE CARAMEL BARS

These are so naughty, but so delicious – not just for the kids, the adults will adore them too. They aren't suitable for freezing.

- Makes 18 bars

> 2 tbsp milk
> 5 x 62.5 g Mars Bars, cut into slices
> 2 tbsp double cream
> 225 g (8 oz) Cornflakes

You will need a small Aga roasting tin (or roasting tin measuring about 30 x 23 cm/ 12 x 9 in), greased.

Pour the milk into a non-stick saucepan, to cover the base. Add half the Mars Bar slices and stir on the simmering plate (or on the hob set to a low heat) until melted. Add the remaining Mars Bar slices and the cream, and stir again until melted. Add the Cornflakes and stir until all the flakes are coated.

Spoon into the prepared tin and level the top with the back of a spoon. Transfer to the fridge to set.

Cut across the long side of the tin in six equal lines, and cut across the short side in three equal lines, to give 18 squares – and enjoy!

Secret

- The milk in the pan stops the Mars Bars from sticking and therefore burning. Also, adding the Mars Bars in batches means they melt more quickly – keep stirring as they melt, so they do not stick.

CHOCOLATE FRIDGE SQUARES

These biscuits evoke great memories from my childhood – we adored making them! When asking friends which recipes I should put in this book, most people mentioned fridge biscuits – so here they are. They aren't suitable for freezing.

- Makes 24 squares

> 200 g (7 oz) dark chocolate
> 450 g (1 lb) digestive biscuits
> 225 g (8 oz) hard margarine or butter
> 50 g (2 oz) caster sugar
> 2 tbsp golden syrup
> 4 tbsp cocoa powder

You will need a small Aga roasting tin (or roasting tin measuring about 30 x 23 cm/ 12 x 9 in), greased.

Break the chocolate into a bowl and sit on the back of the Aga until melted, stirring occasionally. (For a conventional oven, put the chocolate into a bowl and heat gently over a pan of simmering water, stirring until melted.)

Break the biscuits into a poly bag and bash with a rolling pin, until they are fairly fine.

Measure the margarine, sugar and golden syrup into a saucepan and heat on the simmering plate (or on the hob set to a low heat), stirring until the margarine has melted. Stir in the crushed biscuits and cocoa powder. Mix with a wooden spoon until all the biscuits are coated. Tip into the prepared tin, spread out evenly and leave to chill in the fridge for 15 minutes.

Pour the melted chocolate evenly over the top of the biscuit and return to the fridge for the chocolate to set, which takes about an hour. Cut into 24 squares.

Secrets

- Crush the biscuits about the same as you would for a biscuit base for a cheesecake. If the crumbs are too coarse, the squares will crumble.

- For a variation, use the same quantity of white chocolate instead of dark chocolate for the topping.

MARSHMALLOW CRISPIE SQUARES

These are a gooier version of the Mango and chocolate krispies on page 58. Children will adore both! They aren't suitable for freezing. (See the photograph on page 57.)

- Makes 16 squares

> 100 g (4 oz) margarine or butter
> 100 g (4 oz) marshmallows
> 100 g (4 oz) soft toffees
> 200 g (7 oz) Coco Pops

You will need a small Aga roasting tin (or traybake tin measuring 30 x 23 cm/12 x 9 in), lined with cling film.

Measure the margarine, marshmallows and toffees into a large pan and gently heat on the simmering plate (or on the hob set to a low heat). Stir continuously until everything has melted.

Stir in the Coco Pops until evenly coated in the mixture.

Spoon into the prepared tin, spread evenly with the back of a spoon and pack firmly into the tin. Transfer to the fridge for at least an hour, or until set. Tip out of the tin, remove the cling film, and cut into 16 squares.

Secrets

- Wet the inside of the roasting tin with water before lining with cling film, which will help the cling film stick to the sides of the tin.

- Buy any soft, chewy toffee, not the hard ones, otherwise they will take ages to melt.

CHOCOLATE HONEY NUT FLAKES

This recipe is a twist on a classic children's favourite recipe. I use Honey Nut Cornflakes, but if you only have plain cornflakes you can use these too. They aren't suitable for freezing.

- Makes 10 cases

> 50 g (2 oz) margarine or butter
> 2 tbsp drinking chocolate powder
> 1 rounded tbsp golden syrup
> 75 g (3 oz) Honey Nut Cornflakes

Arrange about 10 paper bun cases on a baking sheet.

Measure the margarine into a pan and heat gently on the simmering plate (or on the hob set to a low heat) until melted. Remove from the heat, add the drinking chocolate and golden syrup and stir well until combined.

Add the Honey Nut Cornflakes and stir until completely coated. Then spoon into paper cases and leave to set in the fridge for at least an hour, or until set.

Secret

- If you do not have drinking chocolate, you can use cocoa powder, but you may need to add one teaspoon extra of golden syrup as cocoa is more bitter than drinking chocolate.

Chocolate honey nut flakes (front), Mango and chocolate krispies (centre, see page 58) and Marshmallow crispie squares (back, see page 55)

MANGO AND CHOCOLATE KRISPIES

We all had chocolate crispies as children and this is my updated version. These are different to the Marshmallow crispie squares on page 55 as not only are the ingredients different, but these are white and the others are brown as they use Coco Pops. They aren't suitable for freezing. (See the photograph on page 57.)

- Makes 16 squares

> 200 g (7 oz) white chocolate
> 3 tbsp golden syrup
> 50 g (2 oz) baking margarine, from the fridge
> 100 g (4 oz) Rice Krispies
> 100 g (4 oz) dried mango, snipped into small pieces

You will either need a small Aga roasting tin (or Swiss roll tin measuring 30 x 23 cm/ 12 x 9 in), lined with cling film, or 16 paper bun cases.

Measure the chocolate into a bowl. Add the golden syrup and margarine and sit on the back of the Aga or in the simmering oven until melted, stirring occasionally. (For a conventional oven, put the chocolate, golden syrup and margarine into a bowl and heat gently over a pan of simmering water, stirring until melted.)

Measure the Rice Krispies and mango pieces into a bowl and pour over the melted chocolate mixture, stirring well until all the Krispies are coated.

Spoon into the prepared tin, spread evenly with the back of a spoon and pack firmly into the tin. If using paper cases, shape into 16 balls and put in the cases. Transfer to the fridge for at least an hour, or until set.

Tip out of the tin, remove the cling film and cut into 16 pieces.

Secret
- You can vary the dried fruit as you wish; replace the same quantity of mango with sultanas or other dried fruits.

ORANGE DRIZZLE CAKE

This is a variation on lemon drizzle cake, but I have made it simpler for children as it is just cooked in one tin. It freezes well with its crunchy topping.

- Cuts into 8 wedges

>   100 g (4 oz) soft butter
>   175 g (6 oz) caster sugar
>   175 g (6 oz) self-raising flour
>   1–2 tsp baking powder
>   2 eggs
>   4 tbsp milk
>   Grated rind of 1 large orange

- For the icing

>   About 2 tbsp orange juice
>   175 g (6 oz) granulated sugar

You will need a deep, 20 cm (8 in)-diameter cake tin, greased and base lined with a disc of non-stick baking parchment.

Measure all the ingredients into a large bowl and beat with a wooden spoon until well blended. Turn the mixture into the prepared tin and level the top.

TWO-OVEN AGA Slide the tin onto the lowest set of runners in the roasting oven with the cold sheet on the second set of runners. Bake for about 20 minutes, until golden brown and shrinking away from the sides of the tin.

THREE- AND FOUR-OVEN AGA Slide the tin onto the lowest set of runners in the baking oven and bake for 20–25 minutes. If the cake is getting too brown, slide the cold sheet onto the second set of runners.

CONVENTIONAL OVEN Bake in a preheated oven (180°C/350°F/160°C Fan/Gas 4) for about 20 minutes.

For the icing, mix together the orange juice and sugar to give a runny consistency. Spread out evenly over the hot cake and leave to set.

Secret
- This cake can also be made with lime – use the grated rind of 3 limes and the same quantity of lime juice as orange juice.

MINI PARTY CAKES

Not only will children adore eating these, they are so easy to make and they will love decorating them. They freeze well iced.

- Makes 36 mini cakes

- For the basic mixture

        100 g (4 oz) baking margarine, from the fridge
        100 g (4 oz) caster sugar
        100 g (4 oz) self-raising flour
        1 level tsp baking powder
        2 eggs

- For the icing

        100 g (4 oz) icing sugar
        2 tbsp water
        Sweeties to decorate

You will need a 12-hole mini bun tin, greased or lined with paper cases.

Measure the cake ingredients into a large mixing bowl and beat until smooth. Spoon a third of the mixture into the bun tin or paper cases.

TWO, THREE- AND FOUR-OVEN AGA Slide the tin onto the grid shelf on the floor of the roasting oven and bake for 10–12 minutes, until well risen and golden brown. If the cakes are getting too brown, slide the cold sheet onto the second set of runners. Repeat twice more with the remaining mixture.

CONVENTIONAL OVEN Bake in a preheated oven (180°C/350°F/160°C Fan/Gas 4) for 12–15 minutes. Repeat twice more with the remaining mixture.

Set aside to cool. To make the icing, mix together the icing sugar and water until a fairly stiff paste. Using a teaspoon, spoon a circle of the icing on the top of each bun. Decorate while the icing is still soft with sweeties of your choice (see ideas below).

- Ideas for decoration

        Maltesers
        Smarties
        Jelly Babies
        Dolly Mixtures
        Jelly Tots
        Mini Liquorice Allsorts
        Jelly Beans
        Sultanas

Mini party cakes and Chocolate mini cakes (see page 62)

CHOCOLATE MINI CAKES

This is the same recipe as the Mini party cakes (see page 60), but with added chocolate – use the same white icing as for that particular recipe, it looks stunning on the dark cakes. They freeze well iced. (See the photograph on page 61.)

- Makes 36 mini cakes

> 25 g (1 oz) cocoa powder
> 1 tbsp boiling water
> 100 g (4 oz) baking margarine, from the fridge
> 100 g (4 oz) caster sugar
> 75 g (3 oz) self-raising flour
> 1 level tsp baking powder
> 2 eggs

You will need a 12-hole mini bun tin, greased or lined with paper cases.

Measure the cocoa powder into a large bowl, pour in the boiling water and mix to a smooth paste. Add the remaining cake ingredients and beat until smooth. Spoon a third of the mixture into the bun tin or paper cases.

TWO, THREE- AND FOUR-OVEN AGA Slide the tin onto the grid shelf on the floor of the roasting oven and bake for 10–12 minutes, until well risen and golden brown. If the cakes are getting too brown, slide the cold sheet onto the second set of runners. Repeat twice more with the remaining mixture.

CONVENTIONAL OVEN Bake in a preheated oven (180°C/350°F/160°C Fan/Gas 4) for 12–15 minutes. Repeat twice more with the remaining mixture.

Set aside to cool. To make the icing, mix together the icing sugar and water until a fairly stiff paste. Using a teaspoon, spoon a circle of the icing on the top of each bun. Decorate while the icing is still soft with sweeties of your choice (see page 60).

Variations

- LEMON MINI BUNS Add grated rind of 1 lemon to the basic mix. For the icing, use lemon juice instead of water.
- ORANGE MINI BUNS Add grated rind of 1 orange to the basic mix. For the icing, use orange juice instead of water.
- LIME MINI BUNS Add grated rind of 2 limes to the basic mix. For the icing, use lime juice instead of water.
- CHOCOLATE CHIP MINI BUNS Add 25 g (1 oz) dark chocolate chips to the basic mixture and/or the chocolate mixture.

Secret

- If using paper cases, don't overfill otherwise the mixture will not rise evenly and will get stuck to the sides of the tins – leave a little gap at the top of each case.

LEMON CURD FAIRY CAKES

These will be loved by all – for a variation, use orange or lime curd. They freeze well when filled.

- Makes 12 fairy cakes

> 100 g (4 oz) baking margarine, from the fridge
> 100 g (4 oz) caster sugar
> 100 g (4 oz) self-raising flour
> 1 tsp baking powder
> 2 eggs
> 6 tsp luxury lemon curd

You will need a 12-hole bun tin, greased or lined with paper cases.

Measure all the ingredients except the lemon curd into a bowl and beat with a wooden spoon until combined and smooth. Spoon evenly into the bun tin or paper cases.

TWO-OVEN AGA Slide the tin onto the grid shelf on the floor of the roasting oven with the cold sheet on the second set of runners. Bake for 12–15 minutes, until well risen and golden brown.

THREE- AND FOUR-OVEN AGA Slide the tin onto the grid shelf on the floor of the baking oven and bake for about 15 minutes, until well risen and golden brown.

CONVENTIONAL OVEN Bake in a preheated oven (180°C/350°F/160°C Fan/Gas 4) for about 15 minutes.

Set aside to cool. Once cold, cut out a shallow cone shape vertically from the centre of each fairy cake. Fill each hole with half a teaspoon of lemon curd and return each cone on top of the lemon curd at a slight angle. Dust with icing sugar and serve.

Secret
- Be sure to buy lemon curd that is the real thing – check that the ingredients contain eggs, butter and lemons, and no preservatives.

JAZZY'S GINGERBREAD MEN

You don't often see gingerbread men recipes in books, perhaps because they are a little tricky to do or because they are not in fashion — well, I think they deserve a comeback! You can buy gingerbread men and women cutters from kitchen shops. They freeze well.

- Makes about 10 gingerbread men

    175 g (6 oz) plain flour
    ½ tsp bicarbonate of soda
    75 g (3 oz) light muscovado sugar
    2 tsp ground ginger
    50 g (2 oz) baking margarine, from the fridge
    2 tbsp golden syrup
    ½ egg, beaten

- To decorate
    Fruit (see my secret suggestion, below)

You will need two baking sheets, greased, and a gingerbread man (or woman) cutter.

Measure the flour, bicarbonate of soda, sugar and ginger into a bowl. Using your fingers, rub in the margarine until the mixture resembles fine breadcrumbs. Stir in the golden syrup and egg, mixing to a smooth dough. Roll out the dough on a floured worksurface to about 5 mm (¼ in) thick. Cut out the gingerbread men using the cutter and arrange on the prepared baking sheets. Use the fruit for eyes and buttons.

TWO-, THREE- AND FOUR-OVEN AGA Slide the baking sheets onto the grid shelf on the floor of the roasting oven with the cold sheet on the second set of runners. Bake for 8–10 minutes, until dark golden. Cool a little and then, using a fish slice, carefully lift onto a wire rack.

CONVENTIONAL OVEN Bake in a preheated oven (190°C/375°F/170°C Fan/Gas 5) for about 12 minutes.

Leave to cool completely and enjoy.

Secrets

- It is important not to add too much egg or get the dough too sticky, as it will then be difficult to transfer the gingerbread men to the baking sheet. If you accidentally add too much liquid, knead in a little more flour until it is the consistency of a pastry dough.

- I find it best to roll a quarter of the dough at a time as it is easier to handle and does not get too sticky. You can re-roll the dough as much as you need to.

- It is traditional to decorate the gingerbread men with currants or raisins but you can use all sorts of different things — Smarties, snipped pieces of dried apricots, cranberries, liquorice or nuts (as long as there are no children around with a nut allergy).

Jazzy's gingerbread men (front) and Percy Road flapjacks (back, see page 66)

PERCY ROAD FLAPJACKS

These are always extremely popular with children and are so easy to make. The flapjacks are my original recipe with added ginger, as invented by my lovely friends in Percy Road. They freeze well. (See the photograph on page 65.)

- Cuts into 12 wedges

> 100 g (4 oz) butter
> 100 g (4 oz) demerara sugar
> 100 g (4 oz) golden syrup
> 225 g (8 oz) porridge oats
> 2 tsp ground ginger
> 3 bulbs stem ginger, chopped very finely

You will need a 20 cm (8 in)-diameter loose-bottomed sandwich tin, greased and base lined with a disc of non-stick baking parchment.

Measure the butter, sugar and golden syrup into a medium-sized saucepan and heat gently on the simmering plate (or on the hob set to a low heat) until the butter has melted and the sugar dissolved. Remove the pan from the heat and stir in the rolled oats and ground and chopped ginger.

Turn the mixture into the prepared tin and press down firmly with the back of a spoon to level the surface.

TWO-OVEN AGA Slide the tin onto the grid shelf on the floor of the roasting oven with the cold sheet on the second set of runners. Bake for 10–12 minutes, until golden brown. Take care not to over-bake the flapjacks or they will be very hard.

THREE- AND FOUR-OVEN AGA Slide the tin onto the grid shelf on the floor of the baking oven and bake for 12–15 minutes, until golden brown.

CONVENTIONAL OVEN Bake in a preheated oven (160°C/325°F/140°C Fan/Gas 3) for about 35 minutes.

Loosen the edges of the flapjacks from the sides of the tin then leave to cool in the tin for about 10 minutes. Invert the flapjacks onto a board and slice into 12 wedges. Leave to cool completely on a wire rack.

Secrets
- Cut the flapjack while it is still warm otherwise it will be too hard to cut through.

- If you are not keen on ginger, just leave out the ground and stem ginger and it will still be delicious.

SPICED APRICOT WELSH CAKES

Welsh cakes are perfect on the Aga as they cook straight onto the simmering plate. They are best eaten the day they are made and they freeze well, too. (See the photograph on page 69.)

- Makes 12 Welsh cakes

> 175 g (6 oz) self-raising flour
> 1 tsp baking powder
> 75 g (3 oz) butter, soft
> 50 g (2 oz) caster sugar
> 50 g (2 oz) ready-to-eat dried apricots, snipped into raisin-sized pieces
> ½ tsp mixed spice
> 1 egg beaten with 1 tbsp milk

You will need a 7.5 cm (3 in) scone cutter.

Measure the flour and baking powder into a mixing bowl and rub in the butter until the mixture resembles fine breadcrumbs. Add the sugar, apricots and spice and then gradually add the egg and milk mixture, kneading with your hands until a firm dough has formed.

Lightly flour a work surface and knead the dough lightly. Using a rolling pin, roll out the dough to about 5 mm (¼ in) thick and cut into rounds using the scone cutter.

TWO-, THREE- AND FOUR-OVEN AGA Lift the lid on the simmering plate and allow to cool for a couple of minutes. Cover with non-stick baking parchment or grease the simmering plate with a little sunflower oil.

CONVENTIONAL OVEN Cook on a preheated non-stick griddle pan or frying pan, lightly greased.

Cook the Welsh cakes directly on the simmering plate, griddle pan or frying pan, for about 3 minutes on each side, or until golden brown and cooked through. Sprinkle with caster sugar and serve with butter.

Secrets

- Traditionally, sweet doughs should be cut with a fluted cutter, but I find a plain cutter easier for Welsh cakes because of the fruit in the dough.

- Do not cook too fast as the outsides will become too crisp and the middle will not be cooked.

SULTANA DROP SCONES

In the old days, these were made on a solid metal griddle on an open fire. Now it is more practical to use a large non-stick frying pan or, for Aga owners, cook on the simmering plate. They freeze well.

- Makes about 24 drop scones

> 175 g (6 oz) self-raising flour
> 1 tsp baking powder
> 40 g (1½ oz) caster sugar
> 1 egg
> About 200 ml (7 fl oz) milk
> 50 g (2 oz) sultanas
> Little oil

Measure the flour, baking powder and sugar into a mixing bowl. Make a well in the centre and then add the egg and half of the milk. Whisk well until a smooth, thick batter and then beat in enough of the remaining milk to make a batter the consistency of thick cream.

TWO- THREE- AND FOUR-OVEN AGA Lift the lid on the simmering plate for about 3 minutes to cool down a little. Pour a little oil onto kitchen paper and rub onto the simmering plate, or cover with non-stick graphite paper.

CONVENTIONAL OVEN Heat a non-stick frying pan over a high heat and brush lightly with oil.

Drop the mixture in dessertspoonfuls directly onto the simmering plate or frying pan, spacing the mixture well apart to allow for them to spread. When bubbles appear on the surface, turn over the scones with a palette knife and cook on the other side for a further 30 seconds to 1 minute, until they are golden brown.

Lift the pancakes onto a wire rack and cover with a clean tea towel to keep them soft. Continue cooking pancakes with the remaining mixture in the same way. Serve at once with butter and golden or maple syrup.

Secret
- This is when the Aga really comes into its own; cooking on the plate without the need for a frying pan. Don't leave the lid up too long, though, or you will lose a lot of heat from the Aga – just leave long enough for the plate to cool a little so the pancakes do not burn.

Sultana drop scones (right) and Spiced apricot Welsh cakes (left, see page 67)

Coffee shop cakes

Coffee and tea have never been so popular and instead of 'ladies who lunch', it's now very much 'ladies who meet in Starbucks' or 'ladies who latte'! The cakes in this chapter are of the type you would have with your skinny latte or frappucino. The recipes are pretty naughty but simply delicious, and often freeze well, so you'll always have a tantalising treat for the friend popping in on the way back from the gym or the shops.

BLUEBERRY BREAKFAST MUFFINS

Best served warm, these muffins are wonderful for breakfast. Don't expect them to be sweet like a cake as they are more like scones in texture. They freeze well.

- **Makes 12 muffins**

> 300 g (10 oz) plain flour
> 1 tbsp baking powder
> 75 g (3 oz) caster sugar
> Grated rind of 1 lemon
> 2 eggs
> 225 ml (8 fl oz) milk
> 100 g (4 oz) butter, melted and left to cool
> 1 tsp vanilla extract
> 225 g (8 oz) fresh blueberries
> A little demerara sugar, for sprinkling (optional)

You will need a 12-hole muffin tin, greased or lined with paper cases.

Measure the flour, baking powder, sugar and grated lemon rind into a mixing bowl and stir briefly. Mix together the eggs, milk, butter and vanilla extract and then add these to the dry ingredients. Mix together the ingredients with a wooden spoon or spatula, but don't over-mix. Gently stir in the blueberries and spoon the mixture into the muffin cases or tins, filling almost to the top. Sprinkle each muffin with a little demerara sugar, if using.

TWO-OVEN AGA Slide the tin onto the grid shelf on the floor of the roasting oven with the cold sheet on the second set of runners. Bake for 20–25 minutes, until well risen and golden brown.

THREE- AND FOUR-OVEN AGA Slide the tin onto the grid shelf on the floor of the baking oven and bake for 20–25 minutes. If the muffins are getting too brown, slide the cold sheet onto the second set of runners.

CONVENTIONAL OVEN Bake in a preheated oven (200°C/400°F/180°C Fan/Gas 6) for 20–25 minutes.

Allow the muffins to cool slightly in the tray and then lift out and serve warm. If you have made them ahead and want to reheat them, pop them in the simmering oven for a few minutes until warm.

Secret
- Paper muffin cases are available from good supermarkets or kitchen shops. Be sure to buy muffin cases as these are deeper than bun cases – they are not essential, but they do make life easier when extracting the muffins from the tins!

Blueberry breakfast muffins (left) and Orange and hazelnut muffins (right, see page 74)

ORANGE AND HAZELNUT MUFFINS

These are breakfast-style muffins – orange and hazelnuts are a wonderful combination. They freeze well. (See the photograph on page 73.)

- Makes 12 muffins

> 300 g (10 oz) plain flour
> 1 tbsp baking powder
> 75 g (3 oz) caster sugar
> 2 eggs
> 225 ml (8 fl oz) milk
> 100 g (4 oz) butter, melted and left to cool
> Grated rind of 1 large orange
> 100 g (4 oz) roasted chopped hazelnuts

You will need a 12-hole muffin tin, greased or lined with paper cases.

Measure the flour, baking powder and sugar into a mixing bowl and stir briefly. Mix together the eggs, milk, butter and orange rind and then add these to the dry ingredients. Mix together the ingredients with a wooden spoon or spatula, but don't over-mix. Gently stir in 75 g (3 oz) of the chopped hazelnuts and then spoon the mixture into the muffin cases or tins, filling almost to the top. Sprinkle each muffin with the remaining chopped hazelnuts.

TWO-OVEN AGA Slide the tin onto the grid shelf on the floor of the roasting oven with the cold sheet on the second set of runners. Bake for 20–25 minutes, until well risen and golden brown.

THREE- AND FOUR-OVEN AGA Slide the tin onto the grid shelf on the floor of the baking oven and bake for 20–25 minutes. If the muffins are getting too brown, slide the cold sheet onto the second set of runners.

CONVENTIONAL OVEN Bake in a preheated oven (200°C/400°F/180°C Fan/Gas 6) for 20–25 minutes.

Allow the muffins to cool slightly in the tray and then lift out and serve warm. If you have made them ahead and want to reheat them, pop them in the simmering oven for a few minutes until warm.

Secret
- You can easily buy roasted chopped hazelnuts – they usually come in a 100 g (4 oz) packet. Alternatively, buy whole roasted hazelnuts and chop finely.

PINEAPPLE AND SULTANA BUNS

The pineapple in these buns keeps them really moist and it also makes the perfect combination with a cappuccino. They freeze well.

- Makes 18 buns

    200 g (7 oz) self-raising flour
    150 g (5 oz) butter, soft
    150 g (5 oz) light muscovado sugar
    3 eggs
    1 x 425 g can crushed pineapple in fruit juice
    175 g (6 oz) sultanas
    A little demerara sugar, for sprinkling

You will need two 12-hole bun tins, greased or lined with paper cases.

Measure the flour, butter, sugar and eggs into a mixing bowl and beat with a mixer or wooden spoon until smooth. Drain the pineapple really well in a sieve and pat dry with kitchen paper. Fold the pineapple and sultanas into the mixture and mix evenly. Spoon into the bun tins or paper cases and sprinkle each bun with a little demerara sugar.

TWO-OVEN AGA Slide the tins onto the grid shelf on the floor of the roasting oven for about 20 minutes, until golden brown and firm.

THREE- AND FOUR-OVEN AGA Slide the tins onto the grid shelf on the floor of the baking oven and bake for 20–25 minutes, until golden brown and firm.

CONVENTIONAL OVEN Bake in a preheated oven (180°C/350°F/160°C Fan/Gas 4) for 25–30 minutes.

Allow the muffins to cool slightly in the tray and then lift out. Serve warm or cold.

Secrets
- It is so important for the pineapple to be dried with kitchen paper otherwise it will sink to the bottom of the buns.

- If using paper cases, sit them in a bun or muffin tin to hold their shape during cooking.

PINWHEEL MINCE PIES

These are a real cheat and such a quick alternative to the traditional mince pie – perfect to serve as a biscuit with coffee around Christmas time. They freeze well.

- Makes 18 mince pies

> 1 x 375 g packet ready rolled shortcrust pastry
> 1 x 410 g jar mincemeat
> A little milk for glazing
> 25 g (1 oz) flaked almonds
> Icing sugar, for dusting

You will need a baking sheet, greased and lined with non-stick baking parchment.

Unroll the pastry and lay it flat on a floured work surface. Roll again so it is a little bigger to about 36 x 32 cm (14 x 13 in). Spread the mincemeat over the pastry, leaving a 2 cm (¾ in) border along the longest edges. Tightly roll in one of the long edges and continue rolling up the pastry tightly, in a cigar shape. Brush a little milk along the remaining long edge so the pastry seals with the roll. Wrap in cling film and chill for about 30 minutes.

Cut across the roll into thin rounds, giving you about 18 circles. Lie them on the prepared baking sheet, evenly spaced. Flatten each circle slightly with the palm of your hand and sprinkle with flaked almonds.

Two-, three- and four-oven AGA Slide the baking sheet onto the grid shelf on the floor of the roasting oven and bake for 12–15 minutes, until golden brown and the pastry is cooked (take care not to overcook otherwise the fruit will burn).

Conventional oven Bake in a preheated oven (200°C/400°F/180°C Fan/Gas 6) for 15–20 minutes.

Allow to cool slightly, dust with icing sugar and serve.

Secrets
- Ready rolled shortcrust pastry is a great cheat. I roll it again so that the pastry is not too thick and so will cook in time before burning the fruit. You can buy standard shortcrust or sweet shortcrust or, of course, you can make your own.

- If you have a nut allergy, omit the flaked almonds – the pies will still be delicious.

Pinwheel mince pies (left) and Almond and cherry slice (right, see page 78)

ALMOND AND CHERRY SLICE

This is a thin slice because, as it is full of flavour, it should not be too thick and rich. The flavour is similar to a Bakewell tart but with cherry instead of raspberry jam – of course, you could use raspberry jam if you prefer. It isn't suitable for freezing. (See the photograph on page 77.)

- Cuts into 12 slices

>   100 g (4 oz) butter, very soft
>   50 g (2 oz) caster sugar
>   100 g (4 oz) plain flour
>   1 tsp almond extract
>   6 tbsp black cherry jam
>   50 g (2 oz) glacé cherries, rinsed, dried and cut into quarters
>   100 g (4 oz) golden marzipan
>   50 g (2 oz) almond slithers

You will need a small Aga roasting tin (or roasting tin measuring about 30 x 23 cm/ 12 x 9 in), lined with foil and greased.

Measure the butter and sugar into a mixing bowl and beat with a wooden spoon until pale and fluffy. Stir in the flour and almond extract and beat to make a soft pastry-like dough. Press the mixture into the base of the prepared tin, spreading out evenly with the back of a spoon.

Mix together the jam and cherries and spread over the dough, within 5 cm (2 in) of the edges. Coarsely grate the marzipan and sprinkle over the jam. Finally sprinkle over the almond slithers.

Two-, three- and four-oven Aga Slide the tin onto the grid shelf on the floor of the roasting oven, with the cold sheet on the second set of runners. Bake for about 20 minutes, until golden brown.

Conventional oven Bake in a preheated oven (180°C/350°F/160°C Fan/Gas 4) for 25–30 minutes.

Leave in the tin until almost cold, then peel off the foil and cut into 12 slices.

Secret
- Almond slithers can be bought in all good supermarkets; they are the whole almond cut into thin slices and look very attractive. If you cannot find them, you can carefully cut your own from whole almonds or used flaked almonds instead.

SCOTTISH GINGER SHORTBREAD

I use semolina in my shortbread to give a lovely crunch, but if you haven't got any, you can use cornflour instead. It freezes well.

• Makes 12 shortbread wedges

> 175 g (6 oz) plain flour
> 175 g (6 oz) butter, at room temperature
> 75 g (3 oz) caster sugar
> 75 g (3 oz) semolina
> 1 tsp ground ginger
> 4 bulbs stem ginger, cut into raisin-sized pieces
> A little demerara sugar, for sprinkling

You will need a 20 cm (8 in)-diameter cake tin.

Measure the flour, butter, caster sugar, semolina and ground ginger into a food processor and process until the mixture is thoroughly combined and comes together to form a dough. This can also be done by hand, rubbing the butter into the flour first and then adding the sugar and semolina, working the ingredients together to form a ball of mixture.

Press half the shortbread mixture into the tin and level with the back of a spoon. Sprinkle over the ginger pieces and press the remaining mixture over the ginger, levelling with the back of a spoon. Sprinkle the top with the demerara sugar.

TWO-OVEN AGA Slide the tin onto the lowest set of runners in the roasting oven, with the cold sheet on the second set of runners. Bake for about 20 minutes, until pale golden. Transfer to the simmering oven for a further 45 minutes, until firm.

THREE- AND FOUR-OVEN AGA Slide the tin onto the lowest set of runners in the baking oven and bake for about 45 minutes, until pale golden and firm. If the shortbread is getting too brown, slide the cold sheet onto the second set of runners.

CONVENTIONAL OVEN Bake in a preheated oven (160°C/325°F/140°C Fan/Gas 3) for 30–40 minutes.

Allow the shortbread to cool in the tin for a few minutes and then cut into 12 wedges and leave to cool in the tin. Once stone cold, carefully lift out of the tin onto a wire rack.

Secrets
• There is no need to grease or line the tin before baking as there is plenty of butter in the biscuit, therefore it will not stick.

• Store shortbread in a tin lined with kitchen paper, which will prevent the shortbread going soggy.

APRICOT MARMALADE SPONGE CAKE

You can use apricot jam or marmalade for this recipe, either of which gives a wonderful flavour. It freezes well iced or un-iced.

- Cuts into 8 wedges

> 100 g (4 oz) caster sugar
> 100 g (4 oz) baking margarine, from the fridge
> 175 g (6 oz) self-raising flour
> 2 eggs
> 100 g (4 oz) ready-to-eat dried apricots, snipped into raisin-sized pieces
> 1 tsp baking powder
> 1 rounded tbsp apricot jam or orange marmalade

- For the glaze

> 2 tbsp apricot jam or orange marmalade
> 1 tbsp water

You will need a deep 20 cm (8 in)-diameter cake tin, greased and base lined with a disc of non-stick baking parchment.

Measure all the ingredients into a bowl and beat with a wooden spoon until smooth. Spoon into the prepared tin and level the top.

TWO-OVEN AGA Slide the tin onto the grid shelf on the floor of the roasting oven with the cold sheet on the second set of runners. Bake for 25–30 minutes, until well risen and golden brown.

THREE- AND FOUR-OVEN AGA Slide the tin onto the grid shelf on the floor of the baking oven and bake for about 30 minutes, until well risen and golden brown. If the cake is getting too brown, slide the cold sheet onto the second set of runners.

CONVENTIONAL OVEN Bake in a preheated oven (180°C/350°F/160°C Fan/Gas 4) for 30–35 minutes.

Set aside to cool.

For the glaze, measure the jam or marmalade and water into a pan, whisk until smooth and allow to boil for a minute or so until smooth and glazing consistency. Remove the cake from the tin and spread the glaze over the top of the cake.

Secret
- Don't be tempted to add too much jam or marmalade to the cake mixture as this alters the proportion of the sugar and will result in an unsuccessful cake.

SWEDISH APPLE CAKE

I was given this recipe by Sue, one of my sisters-in-law, and she had been given it by a Swedish friend of hers – so I thank her for this delicious cake. You can also serve it warm with cream or custard as a dessert. It freezes well.

* Cuts into 8–10 wedges

> 225 g (8 oz) butter, softened
> 225 g (8 oz) caster sugar
> 3 eggs
> 350 g (12 oz) plain flour
> 1 tsp baking powder
> 300 ml (½ pint) single cream
> 3 small dessert apples
> 2 tbsp demerara sugar

You will need a deep, 23 cm (9 in)-diameter cake tin or springform tin, greased and base lined with a disc of non-stick baking parchment.

Measure the butter and sugar into a mixing bowl and beat with a wooden spoon until creamed together. Gradually add the eggs, beating as added. Beat in the flour, baking powder and cream and mix until combined.

Peel the apples and remove the core. Cut each apple into eight wedges. Spoon half the cake mixture into the tin and scatter the apple wedges over the top. Spoon over the remaining cake mixture and level the top. Sprinkle with the demerara sugar.

TWO-OVEN AGA Slide the tin onto the grid shelf on the floor of the roasting oven with the cold sheet on the second set of runners. Bake for 30–35 minutes, until golden brown. Transfer the now hot cold sheet to the simmering oven and sit the cake on top. Continue to bake for a further 15 minutes, until well risen and when a skewer comes out clean when inserted into the centre of the cake.

THREE- AND FOUR-OVEN AGA Slide the tin onto the grid shelf on the floor of the baking oven and bake for about 30 minutes. When golden brown, slide the cold sheet onto the second set of runners and continue to bake for a further 10 minutes.

CONVENTIONAL OVEN Bake in a preheated oven (180°C/350°F/160°C Fan/Gas 4) for about 45 minutes.

Run a palette knife around the edges of the cake and set aside to cool. Remove the baking parchment and cool completely on a wire rack.

Secret

* You can use the same quantity of cooking apples if you like; they will be softer than dessert apples and will lose their shape slightly, but they will be just as delicious.

BANANA AND DATE LOAF

This banana loaf is moist and the dates give a lovely texture and sweetness. It freezes well.

- Cuts into 8 slices

> 1 ripe banana
> 1 tbsp milk
> 50 g (2 oz) baking margarine, from the fridge
> 75 g (3 oz) caster sugar
> 100 g (4 oz) plain flour
> 1 tsp bicarbonate of soda
> ½ tsp baking powder
> 1 egg
> 50 g (2 oz) stoned dried dates, chopped into raisin-sized pieces

You will need a 450 g (1 lb) loaf tin, greased and lined with non-stick baking parchment.

Peel the banana and mash in a mixing bowl. Add the rest of the ingredients and mix with a wooden spoon until combined.

TWO-OVEN AGA Slide the tin onto the grid shelf on the floor of the roasting oven with the cold sheet on the second set of runners. Bake for 25–30 minutes, until risen and golden brown. Transfer the now hot cold sheet to the simmering oven and sit the loaf tin on top. Continue to bake for a further 20 minutes, until well risen and a skewer comes out clean when inserted into the centre of the cake.

THREE- AND FOUR-OVEN AGA Slide the tin onto the grid shelf on the floor of the roasting oven and bake for about 20 minutes, until golden brown. Slide the cold sheet onto the second set of runners and continue to bake for a further 20 minutes.

CONVENTIONAL OVEN Bake in a preheated oven (160°C/325°F/140°C Fan/Gas 3) for about 45 minutes.

Run a palette knife around the edge of the loaf and leave to cool in the tin.

Secret
- This cake can be served with a little butter if liked. The dates give a wonderful speckled texture to the inside of the cake.

CINNAMON CAPPUCCINO CAKE

The combination of cinnamon and coffee gives a wonderful caramel flavour. It freezes well un-iced.

- Cuts into 8 wedges

> 1 tbsp instant coffee
> 2 tsp boiling water
> 100 g (4 oz) baking margarine, from the fridge
> 100 g (4 oz) caster sugar
> 100 g (4 oz) self-raising flour
> 2 tsp baking powder
> 4 eggs
> 2 tsp cinnamon powder

- For the cappuccino icing

> 150 ml (¼ pint) double cream, whipped
> 2 tsp instant coffee, dissolved in 1½ tsp boiling water
> 2 tsp icing sugar
> Cinnamon powder, for dusting

You will need two 20 cm (8 in)-diameter loose-bottomed sandwich tins, each greased and base lined with a disc of non-stick baking parchment.

Measure all the ingredients into a bowl or mixer and beat until smooth. Spoon evenly into the prepared tins and level the tops.

TWO-OVEN AGA Slide the tins onto the grid shelf on the floor of the roasting oven with the cold sheet on the second set of runners. Bake for 20–25 minutes, until well risen and golden brown.

THREE- AND FOUR-OVEN AGA Slide the tins onto the grid shelf on the floor of the baking oven and bake for 25–30 minutes, until well risen and golden brown. If the cake is getting too brown, slide the cold sheet onto the second set of runners.

CONVENTIONAL OVEN Bake in a preheated oven (180°C/350°F/160°C Fan/Gas 4) for 20–25 minutes.

Set aside to cool and then turn out of the tin.

For the icing, mix together the ingredients until smooth. Turn one cake upside down onto a plate and spread with half the icing. Then sit the other cake on top and spread the top with the remaining icing. Dust with a little cinnamon to serve.

Secret
- Taste the raw cake mixture and icing and add a little more dissolved coffee if you like it stronger.

WALNUT BUTTERMILK CAKE

I use buttermilk for this recipe as it gives a lovely creamy texture to the cake. The cake freezes well unfilled.

- Cuts into 6–8 wedges

> 250 g (9 oz) self-raising flour
> 2 tsp ground cinnamon powder
> 150 g (5 oz) caster sugar
> 50 g (2 oz) walnuts, coarsely chopped
> 50 g (2 oz) sultanas
> 150 ml (¼ pint) sunflower oil
> 1 tsp baking powder
> 1 tsp bicarbonate of soda
> 1 egg
> 1 x 284 ml carton of buttermilk

- For the filling

> 100 g (4 oz) butter, softened
> 100 g (4 oz) icing sugar
> 1 tsp ground cinnamon powder

You will need two 20 cm (8 in)-diameter loose-bottomed cake tins, each greased and base lined with a disc of non-stick baking parchment.

Measure all the cake ingredients into a mixing bowl and beat with a wooden spoon until combined. Spoon into the prepared tins.

TWO-OVEN AGA Slide the tins onto the grid shelf on the floor of the roasting oven with the cold sheet on the second set of runners. Bake for 30–35 minutes, until golden brown and shrinking away from the sides of the tin.

THREE- AND FOUR-OVEN AGA Slide the tins onto the grid shelf on the floor of the baking oven and bake for about 40 minutes, until golden brown and shrinking away from the sides of the tin. Check after 20 minutes and if the cake is getting too brown, slide the cold sheet onto the second set of runners.

CONVENTIONAL OVEN Bake in a preheated oven (180°C/350°F/160°C Fan/Gas 4) for 35–40 minutes.

Remove from the oven and leave to cool in the tins. To make the filling, mix together the ingredients in a bowl and beat until smooth. Invert one cake onto a plate, spread with the filling and sit the other cake on top.

Secret

- Buttermilk was originally the liquid left behind during butter making when the butter was taken from the top of the mixture. Nowadays, it is a product in its own right and is a slightly soured pasteurised milk.

HOGS LEMON BUNDT CAKE

What is a bundt cake, you may ask? Well, I asked my lovely eldest niece Hannah the same thing when she suggested I put one in the book! A bundt cake is 'a cake with a hole in the middle', or at least that is the American translation (Hannah heard of it from a film!); we would call it a ring mould or the French would say a savarin mould. The American word 'bundt' is taken from the German word 'bundkuchen', which is a German coffee cake. Anyway, it is easy to make and impressive. It freezes well.

- Cuts into 8–10 slices

    175 g (6 oz) baking margarine, from the fridge
    175 g (6 oz) caster sugar
    255 g (8 oz) self-raising flour
    1½ tsp baking powder
    3 eggs
    2 tbsp lemon juice
    Finely grated rind of 1 large lemon

- For the lemon icing

    150 g (5 oz) icing sugar
    2 tbsp lemon juice

You will need a 23 cm (9 in)-diameter garland ring mould of about 1.2 litres (2 pints) capacity, greased and lined with non-stick baking parchment (see my secret tip, opposite).

Measure all the cake ingredients together in a bowl and beat well using a wooden spoon; you can do this in a mixer if you prefer. Spoon evenly into the prepared mould and level the top.

TWO-OVEN AGA Slide the ring mould onto the grid shelf on the floor of the roasting oven with the cold sheet on the second set of runners. Bake for 30–35 minutes, until golden brown, shrinking away from the sides of the ring mould and springy to the touch.

THREE- AND FOUR-OVEN AGA Slide the ring mould onto the lowest set of runners in the baking oven and bake for about 35 minutes, until golden brown, shrinking away from the sides of the ring mould and springy to the touch. If the cake is getting too brown, slide the cold sheet onto the second set of runners.

CONVENTIONAL OVEN Bake in a preheated oven (180°C/350°F/160°C Fan/Gas 4) for 40–45 minutes.

Set aside to cool. Run a palette knife around the outer and inner edges of the tin. Invert the cake onto a plate and remove the baking parchment. If you have any juice left in the lemon, squeeze it over the cake to keep moist (this is not essential).

To make the icing, mix together the icing sugar and lemon juice in a bowl until blended and stiff (the icing is thick to prevent it from running off the cake). Fit a piping bag with a 5 mm (¼ in) star nozzle and fill the bag with icing. Pipe thick 'V' shapes across the cold cake,

about 4 cm (2¼ in) apart and piping from the inner ring to the outer edge. If you are not keen on piping, drizzle the icing over the cake using a teaspoon. Set aside to set.

Cut into wedges on either side of each piped icing chevron.

Secret
- Lining a ring mould can be quite tricky, but it is essential for the cake to come out easily and for the top of the cake to be a perfect shape. Grease the tin well, across the base and inner and outer sides. Cut pieces of baking parchment into squares and lie flat along the base and so they come up the sides slightly. When running the palette knife around the edges of the tin, it will reach the baking parchment and therefore the cake will be released and turn out easily.

PEACH YOGHURT CAKE

This is quite an unusual cake, but will be loved by all. A yoghurt cake has the texture of Madeira cake, which I adore. It freezes well unfilled and un-iced.

- Cuts into 6–8 wedges

> 75 g (3 oz) butter, soft
> 300 g (10 oz) caster sugar
> 3 eggs, separated
> Finely grated rind of 1 orange
> 1 x 125 g pot peach yoghurt
> 225 g (8 oz) self-raising flour

- For the peach icing

> 1 x 125 g pot peach yoghurt
> 150 ml (5 oz) double cream, whipped until stiff
> 75 g (3 oz) dried peaches or 2 fresh peaches, thinly sliced

You will need two 20 cm (8 in)-diameter loose-bottomed cake tins, each greased and base lined with a disc of non-stick baking parchment.

Measure the butter, sugar, egg yolks, orange rind and yoghurt into a large mixing bowl and beat with a wooden spoon or electric hand whisk until smooth.

Whisk the egg whites until stiff like cloud. Stir one spoonful of egg white into the cake mixture and mix in. Then cut and fold the remaining egg whites into the mixture, taking care not to knock the air out of the whites. Sieve in the flour and gently stir into the cake mixture. Spoon evenly into the prepared tins, levelling the top.

TWO-OVEN AGA Slide the tins onto the grid shelf on the floor of the roasting oven with the cold sheet on the second set of runners. Bake for about 20 minutes, until golden brown and shrinking away from the sides of the tin.

THREE- AND FOUR-OVEN AGA Slide the tins onto the lowest set of runners of the baking oven and bake for about 20 minutes, until golden brown and shrinking away from the sides of the tin. If the cake is getting too brown, slide the cold sheet onto the second set of runners.

CONVENTIONAL OVEN Bake in a preheated oven (180°C/350°F/160°C Fan/Gas 4) for 20–25 minutes.

Leave to cool in the tins then turn out and remove the baking parchment. For the icing, mix together the yoghurt and whipped cream and then fold in half the peach slices. Spoon half the icing onto one cake and spread to the edges. Sit the other cake on top and spread the remaining icing over the top. Garnish with the remaining peach slithers and transfer to the fridge until serving.

Secret

- You can vary this recipe as you wish using the same amount of a different flavoured yoghurt and fresh or dried fruit. Do not change the weights, though, only the flavour of yoghurt.

LIME POLENTA CAKE

This is an unusual cake as it uses gluten-free polenta, which is textured, so the cake has little grains in it. It is also moist due to the marmalade and lime juice. It freezes well.

- Cuts into 8–10 wedges

> 2 limes
> 200 g (8 oz) butter, soft
> 250 g (9 oz) caster sugar
> 2 tbsp sunflower oil
> 4 eggs
> 150 g (5 oz) self-raising flour
> 1 tsp baking powder
> 100 g (4 oz) polenta flour or fine polenta
> 100 g (4 oz) lime marmalade, plus extra for glazing

You will need a deep, 23 cm (9 in)-diameter cake tin or springform tin, greased and base lined with a disc of non-stick baking parchment.

Finely grate the rind of the limes and squeeze 2 tablespoons of juice. Measure all the ingredients for the cake into a large mixing bowl and beat with a wooden spoon or electric hand whisk until smooth. Transfer to the prepared tin and smooth the surface.

TWO-OVEN AGA Slide the tin onto the grid shelf on the floor of the roasting oven with the cold sheet on the second set of runners. Bake for about 20 minutes, until golden brown on top. Transfer the now hot cold sheet into the simmering oven and sit the cake on top. Continue to bake for a further 50 minutes, until set on top and golden brown.

THREE- AND FOUR-OVEN AGA Slide the tin onto the grid shelf on the floor of the baking oven and bake for about 30 minutes, until golden brown. Slide the cold sheet onto the second set of runners and continue to bake for a further 30 minutes, until it is set on top and golden brown.

CONVENTIONAL OVEN Bake in a preheated oven (160°C/325°F/140°C Fan/Gas 3) for about an hour.

Set aside, run a palette knife around the edge of the cake and leave to cool. For the glaze, heat the marmalade in a small pan on the simmering plate (or on the hob set to a low heat). If it's too thick, add a little water and whisk until smooth. Remove the cake from the tin and brush with the warmed lime marmalade to glaze.

Secret

- Polenta is the Italian name for fine cornmeal, which can be called polenta flour or fine polenta – look for the fine, instant, quick-cook polenta.

Cupcakes & cookies

Cupcakes are all the rage at the moment; you see stalls full of them at farmers' markets and in high-end wedding stores — iced and piled high rather than having the classic wedding cake. I have made the recipes easy to make at home, and so versatile in terms of flavourings and decoration.

ORANGE AND CHOCOLATE CUPCAKES

These are too good to miss! They are full of flavour and very easy to make. They freeze well iced.

- Makes 12 cupcakes

    25 g (1 oz) cocoa powder
    3 tbsp boiling water
    100 g (4 oz) baking margarine, from the fridge
    100 g (4 oz) caster sugar
    75 g (3 oz) self-raising flour
    1 tsp baking powder
    2 eggs
    Finely grated rind of 1 orange
    Few strips of orange rind for decoration

- For the icing

    100 g (4 oz) orange-flavoured chocolate
    2 tbsp double cream

You will need a 12-hole muffin tin, lined with paper cases.

Measure the cocoa powder into a large mixing bowl and mix with the water to a smooth paste. Add all the remaining ingredients to the bowl and beat until combined and smooth. Spoon evenly into the paper cases.

TWO-OVEN AGA Slide the tin onto the grid shelf on the floor of the roasting oven with the cold sheet on the second set of runners. Bake for 12–15 minutes, until well risen and dark brown.

THREE- AND FOUR-OVEN AGA Slide the tin onto the grid shelf on the floor of the baking oven and bake for about 15 minutes, until well risen and dark brown.

CONVENTIONAL OVEN Bake in a preheated oven (180°C/350°F/160°C Fan/Gas 4) for about 15 minutes.

Leave to cool.

For the icing, break the chocolate into a bowl, and pour over the cream and then sit on the back of the Aga until melted, stirring occasionally. (For a conventional oven, put the chocolate and cream into a bowl and heat gently over a pan of simmering water, stirring until melted.) Spoon the chocolate icing over the cold cakes and level the top.

Decorate with orange rind before the icing sets and transfer to the fridge to set. See page 101 for other decoration ideas.

Secret
- To get lovely curls of orange rind, use a zester or cut a thin slice of orange skin from the orange using a small, sharp knife and cut into needle-thin strips.

LEMON YOGHURT CUPCAKES

I adore yoghurt cake so thought I would invent mini ones, which are just as delicious
– I have made these in bun tins rather than muffin cases, so they are a little shallower
than the other cupcakes. They freeze well un-iced. (See the photograph on page 95.)

- Makes 12 cupcakes

      100 g (4 oz) self-raising flour
      100 g (4 oz) caster sugar
      2 tbsp cornflour
      2 egg yolks
      1 x 150 g pot natural un-set yoghurt
      Finely grated rind of 2 lemons
      25 g (1 oz) butter, melted

- For the icing

      2 tbsp good lemon curd
      Little lemon rind, cut into thin strips to garnish

You will need a 12-hole bun tin, lined with paper cases.

Measure the flour, sugar and cornflour into a mixing bowl. Then stir in the egg yolks,
yoghurt, lemon rind and melted butter and mix together until smooth.

Spoon into the paper cases to within about 5 mm (¼ in) of the top of each case.

TWO-OVEN AGA Slide the tin onto the grid shelf on the floor of the roasting oven with the
cold sheet on the second set of runners. Bake for 10–12 minutes, until well risen and golden
brown.

THREE- AND FOUR-OVEN AGA Slide the tin onto the grid shelf on the floor of the baking
oven and bake for 12–15 minutes. If the cakes are getting too brown, slide the cold sheet onto
the second set of runners until well risen and golden brown.

CONVENTIONAL OVEN Bake in a preheated oven (180°C/350°F/160°C Fan/Gas 4) for
about 18 minutes.

Leave to cool.

Spoon the lemon curd on top of the cold cakes and level the top. Decorate with a cross of
lemon rind or crystallised mint leaves (see page 101).

Secret
- It is best to used un-set yoghurt for this recipe, as the set yoghurt can be a little grainy
  when mixed.

INDULGENT CHOCOLATE CUPCAKES

Just as you had when you were little – full of chocolate! They freeze well iced.

- Makes 12 cupcakes

  25 g (1 oz) cocoa powder
  3 tbsp boiling water
  100 g (4 oz) baking margarine, from the fridge
  100 g (4 oz) caster sugar
  2 eggs
  75 g (3 oz) self-raising flour
  1 tsp baking powder

- For the icing

  100 g (4 oz) dark chocolate
  2 tbsp single cream

You will need a 12-hole muffin tin, lined with paper cases.

Measure the cocoa powder into a large mixing bowl and mix with the water to a smooth paste. Add all the remaining ingredients to the bowl and beat until combined and smooth. Spoon evenly into the paper cases.

TWO-OVEN AGA Slide the tin onto the grid shelf on the floor of the roasting oven with the cold sheet on the second set of runners. Bake for 12–15 minutes, until well risen and golden brown.

THREE- AND FOUR-OVEN AGA Slide the tin onto the grid shelf on the floor of the baking oven and bake for about 15 minutes, until well risen and golden brown.

CONVENTIONAL OVEN Bake in a preheated oven (180°C/350°F/160°C Fan/Gas 4) for about 15 minutes.

Leave to cool.

For the icing, break the chocolate into a bowl and pour over the cream, sit on the back of the Aga until melted, stirring occasionally. (For a conventional oven, put the chocolate into a bowl and heat gently over a pan of simmering water, stirring until melted.) Spoon the chocolate icing over the cold cakes and transfer to the fridge to set.

For ideas for decoration see page 101.

Secret
- You can use pouring double cream for the icing instead of single cream, if preferred.

Indulgent chocolate cupcakes (front) and Lemon yoghurt cupcakes (centre, see page 93)

LAVENDER CUPCAKES

These cupcakes are so fresh and lavendery – they remind me very much of my wonderful holidays in the south of France. They freeze well un-iced. (See the photograph on page 99.)

- Makes 12 cupcakes

      50 g (2 oz) lavender sprigs, reserving 12 to decorate
      100 g (4 oz) baking margarine, from the fridge
      100 g (4 oz) caster sugar
      2 eggs
      100 g (4 oz) self-raising flour
      1 tsp baking powder

- For the icing

      175 g (6 oz) icing sugar
      3 tbsp water

You will need a 12-hole muffin tin, lined with paper cases.

Reserve 12 small lavender sprigs for decoration and finely chop the remaining lavender.

Measure the chopped lavender and all the other cake ingredients into a bowl or mixer and beat until combined and smooth. Spoon evenly into the paper cases.

TWO-OVEN AGA Slide the tin onto the grid shelf on the floor of the roasting oven with the cold sheet on the second set of runners. Bake for 15–20 minutes, until well risen and golden brown.

THREE- AND FOUR-OVEN AGA Slide the tin onto the grid shelf on the floor of the baking oven and bake for about 20 minutes, until well risen and golden brown.

CONVENTIONAL OVEN Bake in a preheated oven (180°C/350°F/160°C Fan/Gas 4) for about 20 minutes.

Leave to cool. To make the icing, measure the icing sugar into a bowl and mix with the water to give a smooth icing. Spoon over the cold cakes and decorate with reserved sprigs of lavender (or for more ideas, see page 101).

Secret
- When icing cupcakes, it is best to pour the icing on top of the cake and then tip the cupcake so the icing naturally runs around the cake, filling the top, inside the paper case. This gives a smooth shiny finish.

BARBIE PINK RASPBERRY CUPCAKES

I just love the look of these – think of a tea party for a little girl and these are the cakes you would serve! They also look stunning as a wedding cake, arranged in a tier. They freeze well un-iced. (See the photograph on page 99.)

- Makes 12 cupcakes

  100 g (4 oz) fresh raspberries, reserving 12 to decorate
  100 g (4 oz) baking margarine, from the fridge
  100 g (4 oz) caster sugar
  2 eggs
  100 g (4 oz) self-raising flour
  I tsp baking powder

- For the Barbie icing

  175 g (6 oz) icing sugar
  2 tbsp water
  2 tbsp blackcurrant squash

You will need a 12-hole muffin tin, lined with paper cases.

Measure the raspberries (except for those reserved to decorate) and the remaining cake ingredients into a bowl or mixer and beat until combined and smooth. Spoon evenly into the paper cases.

TWO-OVEN AGA Slide the tin onto the grid shelf on the floor of the roasting oven with the cold sheet on the second set of runners. Bake for 15–20 minutes, until well risen and golden brown.

THREE- AND FOUR-OVEN AGA Slide the tin onto the grid shelf on the floor of the baking oven and bake for about 20 minutes, until well risen and golden brown.

CONVENTIONAL OVEN Bake in a preheated oven (180°C/350°F/160°C Fan/Gas 4) for about 20 minutes.

Leave to cool. To make the icing, measure the icing sugar into a bowl and mix with the water and blackcurrant squash to give a smooth icing. Spoon over the cold cakes and spread to the edges. Decorate with one reserved raspberry in the centre of the icing or with a crystallised rose petal (see page 101).

Secret
- Use a full-fat blackcurrant drink rather than a 'light' one as it is in a little pale colour. If you prefer, you can use pink food colouring instead.

ROSE WATER CUPCAKES

These are perfect tiered into a pyramid shape for a wedding cake. Unusual, perhaps, when compared to the traditional fruit cake, but they are all the rage and look wonderfully romantic. They freeze well un-iced.

- Makes 12 cupcakes

> 100 g (4 oz) baking margarine, from the fridge
> 100 g (4 oz) caster sugar
> 175 g (6 oz) self-raising flour
> 1 tsp baking powder
> 2 eggs
> 1 tbsp rose water essence

- For the icing

> 175 g (6 oz) icing sugar
> 3 tbsp rose water essence

You will need a 12-hole muffin tin, lined with paper cases.

Measure all the ingredients into a bowl or mixer and beat until combined and smooth. Spoon evenly into the paper cases.

TWO-OVEN AGA Slide the tin onto the grid shelf on the floor of the roasting oven with the cold sheet on the second set of runners. Bake for 15–20 minutes, until well risen and golden brown.

THREE- AND FOUR-OVEN AGA Slide the tin onto the grid shelf on the floor of the baking oven and bake for about 20 minutes, until well risen and golden brown.

CONVENTIONAL OVEN Bake in a preheated oven (180°C/350°F/160°C Fan/Gas 4) for about 20 minutes.

Leave to cool.

To make the icing, measure the icing sugar into a bowl and mix with the rose water to give a smooth icing. Spoon over the cold cakes and decorate with crystallised rose petals (see page 101).

Secrets
- Rose water essence can be bought from good supermarkets and delis and has a wonderful rose flavour.

- You can also buy orange flower water, to make orange flower cupcakes. Make the recipes exactly as above but replace the rose water with orange flower water.

Rose water cupcakes (front), Lavender cupcakes (middle left, see page 96),
Barbie pink raspberry cupcakes (middle right, see page 97) and Almond and cherry cupcakes (back, see page 100)

ALMOND AND CHERRY CUPCAKES

Almond and cherries are a classic combination and work so well together. They freeze well iced. (See the photograph on page 99.)

- Makes 12 cupcakes

>   75 g (3 oz) glacé cherries, rinsed and dried
>   100 g (4 oz) baking margarine, from the fridge
>   100 g (4 oz) caster sugar
>   2 eggs
>   100 g (4 oz) self-raising flour
>   1 tsp baking powder
>   1 tsp almond extract

- For the icing

>   175 g (6 oz) icing sugar
>   3 tbsp water
>   2 tsp almond extract

You will need a 12-hole muffin tin, lined with paper cases.

Remove six cherries from the weighed cherries, cut in half and set aside for decoration. Cut the remaining cherries into small pieces.

Measure all the remaining ingredients into a bowl and beat until they are combined and smooth. Stir in the cherry pieces and spoon the mixture evenly into the paper cases.

TWO-OVEN AGA Slide the tin onto the grid shelf on the floor of the roasting oven with the cold sheet on the second set of runners. Bake for 15–20 minutes, until risen and golden brown.

THREE- AND FOUR-OVEN AGA Slide the tin onto the grid shelf on the floor of the baking oven and bake for about 20 minutes, until well risen and golden brown.

CONVENTIONAL OVEN Bake in a preheated oven (180°C/350°F/160°C Fan/Gas 4) for about 20 minutes.

Leave to cool.

To make the icing, measure the sugar into a bowl and mix with the water and almond extract to give a smooth icing. Spoon over the cold cakes. Decorate with half a cherry in the centre of the icing or for more ideas, see page 101.

Secret

- Use almond extract and not almond essence – the essence is a fake flavour whereas the extract comes from the real nut.

Ideas for cupcake decorations

Cupcakes are very trendy at the moment – they look stunning decorated in a variety of different ways. Here are a few ideas.

- CRYSTALLISED FLOWERS

  These look particularly good on the pale iced cupcakes. Take any edible flower or herb leaf, such as primroses, rose petals, lavender, lemon balm leaves or mint leaves. Beat an egg white in a bowl with a fork, just enough to froth up. Dip the flower or leaf into the egg white so it is covered all over, then dip into white caster sugar (not granulated sugar as it is too coarse) and the sugar will stick to the egg white. Arrange on baking parchment and sit on the back of the Aga to dry out. The sugar forms a crust and, once dry, the flowers or leaves can be used to decorate.

- FRUIT

  Decorate the cupcakes with fresh fruit, such as raspberries, strawberries or blueberries. Alternatively, crystallise the fruit or slices of lemon, lime or orange as above or half dip the fruit in melted white or dark chocolate. Arrange on baking parchment to set hard.

- SHINY GLAZE

  For really shiny glaze icing for the cupcakes, dip the cakes in melted chocolate and leave to set. Do not touch the icing otherwise it will not be smooth. Alternatively, dip the cakes in royal icing (see pages 136–7), which also has a lovely shine to it.

- CHOCOLATE DECORATIONS

  Sprinkle with crumbled Flake bars, Minstrel sweets, chocolate buttons, mini eggs, shavings of chocolate – they look stunning if using contrasting colours, such as white chocolate buttons on Indulgent Chocolate Cupcakes (see page 94). See also page 51 for making chocolate shapes.

- SPARKLE

  Cupcakes decorated in this way look wonderful – put a cup full of granulated white sugar (not caster as it is too fine) into a poly bag and add a drop of food colouring. Shake the bag about and then sprinkle the coloured sugar over iced cupcakes to give a lovely sparkle.

Most glacé icing can have a drop or two of food colouring added to it to give you the desired colour that you want. Go easy on the food colouring, though, as it can be very strong in colour.

BELLS BISCUITS

These are a crispy biscuit with a fresh flavour of orange and lemon – I've named the biscuits after the nursery rhyme: '"Oranges and Lemons", say the Bells of St Clements'. They freeze well.

- Makes about 40 biscuits

> 175 g (6 oz) unsalted butter, softened
> Finely grated rind of 1 lemon and 1 tbsp lemon juice
> Finely grated rind of 1 orange and 1 tbsp orange juice
> 100 g (4 oz) caster sugar
> 225 g (8 oz) plain flour
> About 25 g (1 oz) demerara sugar

You will need three baking sheets, greased.

Measure the butter, lemon rind and juice, orange rind and juice and caster sugar into a mixing bowl and beat with a wooden spoon until light and fluffy. Stir in the flour, bringing the mixture together with your hands and kneading lightly until smooth.

Divide the mixture into two and roll out to form two 15 cm (6 in)-long sausage shapes. Roll the 'sausages' in the demerara sugar to evenly coat. Wrap in non-stick baking parchment or foil and chill in the fridge for about 30 minutes until firm.

Cut each 'sausage' into about 20 slices, 5 mm (¼ in) thick, and put onto the prepared baking sheets, allowing a little room for them to spread.

TWO-OVEN AGA Slide the baking sheets onto the grid shelf on the floor of the roasting oven with the cold sheet on the second set of runners. Bake for 10–12 minutes, until pale golden brown.

THREE- AND FOUR-OVEN AGA Slide the baking sheets onto the grid shelf on the floor of the baking oven and bake for 12–15 minutes. If the biscuits are getting too brown, slide the cold sheet onto the second set of runners.

CONVENTIONAL OVEN Bake in a preheated oven (160°C/325°F/140°C Fan/Gas 3) for 10–12 minutes.

Lift the biscuits off the tray with a fish slice and leave to cool on a wire rack.

Secrets

- The butter must be soft, but not oily. Leave at room temperature to soften as this will make it easier to make the dough.

- Be accurate when you measure the orange and lemon juice, because if you add too much, the dough will be wet and the biscuits will spread too much.

- Wrap the rolled biscuit in foil or baking parchment and not cling film otherwise the roll will sweat and be oily.

CRANBERRY OAT CRUNCHIES

These are the crunchiest biscuits you will ever eat! They are perfect with a cup of coffee on a Sunday morning. They freeze well.

• Makes 14 biscuits

> 90 g (3½ oz) butter, softened
> 75 g (3 oz) light muscovado sugar
> 1 tsp vanilla extract
> 75 g (3 oz) dried cranberries, halved
> 50 g (2 oz) plain flour
> 75 g (3 oz) porridge oats
> ½ tsp bicarbonate of soda

You will need two baking sheets, greased.

Measure the butter and sugar together in a bowl and beat with a wooden spoon until creamed and fluffy. Then stir in the remaining ingredients until all combined.

Shape into 14 walnut-sized balls and arrange on the prepared baking sheets. Flatten slightly.

TWO-OVEN AGA Slide the baking sheets onto the grid shelf on the floor of the roasting oven with the cold sheet on the second set of runners. Bake for 10–12 minutes, until golden brown.

THREE- AND FOUR-OVEN AGA Slide the baking sheets onto the grid shelf on the floor of the baking oven and bake for about 15 minutes, until golden brown. If the crunchies are getting too dark, slide the cold sheet onto the second set of runners.

CONVENTIONAL OVEN Bake in a preheated oven (180°C/350°F/160°C Fan/Gas 4) for 15–18 minutes.

Transfer to a wire rack to cool and store in an airtight tin.

Secret
• For a variation, replace the cranberries with the same quantity of other dried fruits, such as raisins, sultanas and snipped apricots.

SPICED CHRISTMAS STARS

Children love making these and everyone adores eating them. Hang from the Christmas tree for an edible decoration. They freeze well.

- Makes 20 biscuits

> 100 g (4 oz) caster sugar
> 100 g (4 oz) runny honey
> 75 g (3 oz) butter
> 1 tbsp orange juice
> 300 g (10 oz) plain flour
> ½ tsp cinnamon
> 1 tsp mixed spice
> 1 egg
> Finely grated rind of 1 small orange

- For the icing

> 100 g (4 oz) icing sugar
> 4 tbsp orange juice

You will need two baking sheets, greased, and a star cutter and piping bag.

Measure the sugar, honey, butter and orange juice into a pan and gently heat on the simmering plate (or on the hob set to a low heat), stirring all the time, until the sugar has dissolved. Set aside to cool.

Measure the flour, spices, egg and orange rind into a mixing bowl and pour in the cooled liquid. Beat with a wooden spoon until a smooth dough. Tip the dough onto a work surface and knead until smooth. Wrap it in cling film and transfer to the fridge to firm up.

Once the dough is firm, roll out to about 5 mm (¼ in) thick and press out star shapes using a cutter. Re-roll any excess dough and cut out stars, until all is used. Arrange on the prepared baking sheet.

TWO-, THREE- AND FOUR-OVEN AGA Slide the baking sheet onto the grid shelf on the floor of the roasting oven with the cold sheet on the second set of runners. Bake for 10–12 minutes, until golden brown and just cooked.

CONVENTIONAL OVEN Bake in a preheated oven (200°C/400°F/180°C Fan/Gas 6) for 12–15 minutes.

Set aside to cool before removing from the tray.

To make the icing, mix the icing sugar with the orange juice until it is a smooth pipeable paste. Spoon into a piping bag and pipe pretty shapes onto the cold stars.

Secret
- If serving these to adults, replace the orange juice in the biscuit mixture with rum or brandy.

DOUBLE CHOCOLATE CHIP COOKIES

These are delicious crunchy biscuits with chocolate chips. They freeze well.

- Makes 18 biscuits

> 100 g (4 oz) butter, softened
> 75 g (3 oz) caster sugar
> 75 g (3 oz) light muscovado sugar
> 150 g (5 oz) plain flour
> 1 egg
> 25 g (1 oz) cocoa powder
> 100 g (4 oz) white chocolate chips

You will need two baking sheets, greased.

Cream together the butter and both sugars in a bowl with a wooden spoon, until soft and fluffy. Add the flour, egg and cocoa powder and mix for a few moments until a dough ball. Turn out of the bowl onto a work surface and knead in the chocolate chips.

Shape into 18 round balls and arrange on the baking sheets. Press the balls down to about 1 cm (½ in) thick.

TWO-OVEN AGA Slide the baking sheets onto the grid shelf on the floor of the roasting oven with the cold sheet on the second set of runners. Bake for about 15 minutes, until nearly firm and mahogany brown.

THREE- AND FOUR-OVEN AGA Slide the baking sheets onto the grid shelf on the floor of the roasting oven and bake for about 12 minutes, until nearly firm and mahogany brown. If the cookies are getting too brown, slide the cold sheet onto the second set of runners.

CONVENTIONAL OVEN Bake in a preheated oven (180°C/350°F/160°C Fan/Gas 4) for 10–12 minutes.

Transfer to a wire rack to cool and store in an airtight container.

Secrets

- You can use plain or white chocolate chips for this recipe; I like the contrast of white chocolate with the dark biscuit.

- Any biscuit with egg in will not keep for too long, so eat within a couple of days or freeze.

FRESH BLUEBERRY FLYERS

These biscuits are unusual as they have fresh blueberries in them, but the recipe works well as the blueberries do not dry out and are lovely and squidgy in the biscuit. They freeze well.

- Makes 10 large biscuits

> 100 g (4 oz) butter, softened
> 75 g (3 oz) caster sugar
> 50 g (2 oz) light muscovado sugar
> 1 egg, beaten
> 150 g (5 oz) self-raising flour
> 50 g (2 oz) fresh blueberries

You will need two baking sheets, greased.

Cream together the butter and both sugars in a bowl with a wooden spoon, until soft and fluffy. Gradually add the egg and beat well. Add the flour and mix for a few moments until a dough ball.

Shape into 10 round balls and arrange on the baking sheet, spacing them well apart as the biscuits will spread. Press the balls down with your hand to about 1 cm (½ in) thick and press about four blueberries into each biscuit.

TWO-OVEN AGA Slide the baking sheet onto the grid shelf on the floor of the roasting oven with the cold sheet on the second set of runners. Bake for 10–12 minutes, until nearly firm and golden brown.

THREE- AND FOUR-OVEN AGA Slide the baking sheet onto the grid shelf on the floor of the roasting oven and bake for about 12 minutes, until nearly firm and golden brown. If the biscuits are getting too brown, slide the cold sheet onto the second set of runners.

CONVENTIONAL OVEN Bake in a preheated oven (180°C/350°F/160°C Fan/Gas 4) for 10–12 minutes.

Leave to cool on the tray and then transfer to a wire rack.

Secret
- These biscuits will not keep for a long time because of the egg, and the fresh blueberries will become mouldy, so eat within a day.

MEGA OAT COOKIES

These are so easy to make and kids will love making them, too. You do not need to use jumbo porridge oats, just normal Scotts oats. They freeze well.

• Makes 14 huge cookies

> 175 g (6 oz) self-raising flour
> 75 g (3 oz) porridge oats
> 175 g (6 oz) granulated sugar
> 1 tsp bicarbonate of soda
> 1 tsp baking powder
> 175 g (6 oz) butter
> 2 level tbsp golden syrup

You will need two baking sheets, greased.

Measure the flour, oats, sugar, bicarbonate of soda and baking powder into a mixing bowl.

Measure the butter and golden syrup into a pan and heat on the simmering plate (or on the hob set to a low heat), stirring until the butter has melted and combined with the syrup. Pour into the mixing bowl with the dry ingredients and stir until combined.

Turn out of the bowl onto a work surface and divide into 14 pieces and then shape into dough balls, each about 2 cm (1 in) in diameter. Arrange on the baking sheets, not too close to each other as they spread to at least double their size. Press the tops to flatten a little.

TWO-OVEN AGA Slide the baking sheets onto the grid shelf on the floor of the roasting oven, with the cold sheet on the second set of runners. Bake for 10–15 minutes, until golden brown.

THREE- AND FOUR-OVEN AGA Slide the baking sheets onto the grid shelf on the floor of the baking oven and bake for 10–15 minutes, until golden brown.

CONVENTIONAL OVEN Bake in a preheated oven (180°C/350°F/160°C Fan/Gas 4) for 12–15 minutes.

Leave to cool on the baking sheet.

Secrets
• Sit the tin of golden syrup on the back of the Aga to heat a little as this will make it easier to spoon the syrup from the tin.

• The mixture is not a very firm dough.

Mega oat cookies (front) and Amdolo cookies (back, see page 110)

AMDOLO COOKIES

Here is a delicious cookie with a little gooeyness from the nougat. They freeze well. (See the photograph on page 109.)

- Makes 18 biscuits

> 75 g (3 oz) butter
> 75 g (3 oz) caster sugar
> 75 g (3 oz) light muscovado sugar
> 1 egg, beaten
> 175 g (6 oz) self-raising flour
> 1 x 100 g bar milk Toblerone, roughly chopped into raisin-sized pieces.

You will need three baking sheets, greased, or cook in batches on one sheet.

Measure the butter and sugars into a mixing bowl and cream together until light and fluffy. Beat in the egg, flour and Toblerone pieces.

Spoon six large teaspoons onto each baking sheet, spacing them well apart as they spread.

TWO-OVEN AGA Slide the baking sheets onto the grid shelf on the floor of the roasting oven with the cold sheet on the second set of runners. Bake for 10–12 minutes, until golden brown.

THREE- AND FOUR-OVEN AGA Slide the baking sheets onto the grid shelf on the floor of the baking oven and bake for 12–15 minutes, until golden brown. If the cookies are getting too brown, slide the cold sheet onto the second set of runners.

CONVENTIONAL OVEN Bake in a preheated oven (180°C/350°F/160°C Fan/Gas 4) for 15–18 minutes.

Set aside to cool on the sheets.

Secret
- Using light muscovado sugar gives the cookies a gooey middle. If you don't have any, use all caster sugar instead.

AMARETTI BISCUITS

These are a classic almond biscuit made with egg whites so are very light to eat. I use a teaspoon to spoon the biscuits onto the baking sheet, which makes them very rustic looking. If you prefer them to be exactly the same shape and size, pipe using a 1 cm (½ in) plain nozzle. They aren't suitable for freezing.

- Makes 20 biscuits

> 100 g (4 oz) chopped almonds
> 100 g (4 oz) caster sugar
> 1 tsp almond extract
> 2 egg whites

You will need two baking sheets, greased and lined with non-stick baking parchment.

Measure the almonds, three tablespoons of the sugar and the almond extract into a processor and whiz until combined and the almonds are very fine.

Measure the egg whites into a large mixing bowl or freestanding mixer and whisk until stiff like cloud. Fold in the remaining sugar. Fold in the almond and sugar mixture and stir until combined.

Using a teaspoon, spoon heaped spoonfuls of the mixture onto the prepared baking sheets ensuring they are evenly spaced as they will spread a little.

TWO-, THREE- AND FOUR-OVEN AGA Slide the baking sheets onto the grid shelf on the floor of the roasting oven with the cold sheet on the second set of runners. Bake for 15–20 minutes, until well risen and golden brown. (They look a little like meringues once cooked.)

CONVENTIONAL OVEN Bake in a preheated oven (180°C/350°F/160°C Fan/Gas 4) for about 20 minutes. Turn off the oven and leave to cool in the oven.

Carefully transfer to a wire rack to cool completely and store in an airtight container.

Secrets
- These are perfect to serve with a mousse or ice cream, what I would call a posh biscuit.

- When folding the sugar and almonds into the egg whites, be careful not to mix otherwise the air will be knocked out and the biscuits will be flat once baked.

The healthy option

In this day and age we are all more health-conscious, so this chapter gives variety to cake baking and offers the healthy option. Fruit bars are all the rage, some of which can be made and eaten without any cooking. By its nature, many of the recipes in this chapter contain both fresh and dried fruit, removing some of the guilt from cake baking!

WHOLEMEAL LEMON AND LIME CAKE

I really like this deep cake, it has a nutty taste from the wholemeal flour and with a lemon and lime tang, the flavours are lovely. It freezes well un-iced.

- Cuts into 8 wedges

  225 g (8 oz) baking margarine, from the fridge
  225 g (8 oz) caster sugar
  175 g (6 oz) self-raising flour
  100 g (4 oz) wholemeal plain flour
  2 tsp baking powder
  4 eggs
  grated rind of 2 limes plus 1 tbsp of juice
  grated rind of 1 lemon plus 1 tbsp of juice

- For the icing

  175 g (6 oz) light soft cream cheese
  50 g (2 oz) butter, soft
  100 g (4 oz) icing sugar
  1 tsp vanilla extract

You will need a deep, 20 cm (8 in)-diameter cake tin, greased and base lined with a disc of non-stick baking parchment.

Measure all the cake ingredients into a bowl and mix together until smooth. Pour into the prepared tin and level the top.

TWO-OVEN AGA Slide the tin onto the grid shelf on the floor of the roasting oven with the cold sheet on the second set of runners. Bake for 35–40 minutes, until golden brown and shrinking away from the sides of the tin and springy to the touch.

THREE- AND FOUR-OVEN AGA Slide the tin onto the lowest set of runners in the baking oven and bake for 40–45 minutes, until golden brown and shrinking away from the sides of the tin and springy to the touch. If the cake is getting too brown, slide the cold sheet onto the second set of runners.

CONVENTIONAL OVEN Bake in a preheated oven (180°C/350°F/160°C Fan/Gas 4) for 50 minutes–1 hour.

Leave to cool in the tin.

For the icing, mix together the cream cheese, butter, icing sugar and vanilla extract and beat until smooth. Spread over the cake and, using a fork, make a ridged pattern across the top of the cake.

Secrets

- You can also make this cake using all self-raising flour instead of the wholemeal flour if preferred.

- I have used light cream cheese to keep the calories down, but full-fat cream cheese will work just as well.

HERBAL CRANBERRY TEABREAD

I invented this recipe on a cold Sunday afternoon – while making a herbal tea, my little brain thought it would be good to try a teabread recipe using herbal instead of traditional tea! I love the fruity flavours of the tea and red fruits. It has no fat, so is healthy too. It freezes well.

• Cuts into 20 thin slices

> 100 g (4 oz) dried cranberries
> 100 g (4 oz) dried apricots, snipped into small pieces the size of the cranberries
> 100 g (4 oz) sultanas
> 225 g (8 oz) caster sugar
> 300 ml (10 fl oz) hot red herbal tea, using one teabag
> 300 g (10 oz) self-raising flour
> 1 egg, beaten

You will need a small Aga roasting tin (or roasting tin measuring about 30 x 23 cm/ 12 x 9 in), lined with foil and greased.

Measure the dried fruits and sugar into a bowl and pour over the hot tea. Cover with a tea towel and sit beside the Aga for a minimum of 2 hours for the fruit to plump up.

Add the flour and eggs to the plumped fruit and stir with a wooden spoon until combined. Spoon into the prepared tin and level the top.

TWO-OVEN AGA Slide the tin onto the grid shelf on the floor of the roasting oven with the cold sheet on the second set of runners. Bake for 30–35 minutes, until golden brown and shrinking away from the sides of the tin.

THREE- AND FOUR-OVEN AGA Slide the tin onto the grid shelf on the floor of the baking oven and bake for 35–40 minutes, until golden brown and shrinking away from the sides of the tin. If the teabread is getting too brown, slide the cold sheet onto the second set of runners.

CONVENTIONAL OVEN Bake in a preheated oven (180°C/350°F/160°C Fan/Gas 4) for about 40 minutes.

Set aside to cool in the tin. Once cold, cut into thin slices.

Secret
• After the fruit has soaked, it may not have absorbed all the tea. If this is the case, add the fruit and the tea to the mixing bowl to mix with the other ingredients.

CARROT AND WALNUT CAKE

Here is a classic carrot cake, with the addition of walnuts. I have used wholemeal flour as it has a nutty flavour and therefore complements the walnuts. Use white self-raising flour if preferred. It freezes well un-filled or iced.

- Cuts into 8 wedges

> 150 ml (¼ pint) sunflower oil
> 250 g (9 oz) wholemeal self-raising flour
> 1 tsp baking powder
> 150 g (5 oz) light muscovado sugar
> 1 tsp vanilla extract
> 50 g (2 oz) walnuts, shelled and coarsely chopped
> 150 g (5 oz) carrots, peeled and coarsely grated
> 2 eggs
> 2 tbsp milk

- For the icing

> 225 g (8 oz) low-fat cream cheese
> 2 tbsp icing sugar
> 1 tsp vanilla extract

You will need a deep, 20 cm (8 in)-diameter cake tin, greased and base lined with a disc of non-stick baking parchment.

Measure all the cake ingredients into a large bowl and mix until combined. Spoon into the prepared tin and level the top.

TWO-OVEN AGA Slide the tin onto the grid shelf on the floor of the roasting oven with the cold sheet on the second set of runners. Bake for about 25 minutes, until golden brown. Transfer the now hot cold sheet to the simmering oven and sit the cake on top for a further 15 minutes, until a skewer comes out clean when inserted into the centre of the cake.

THREE- AND FOUR-OVEN AGA Slide the tin onto the grid shelf on the floor of the baking oven and bake for about 20 minutes. Slide in the cold sheet onto the second set of runners and continue to cook for a further 20 minutes, until golden brown and firm to the touch.

CONVENTIONAL OVEN Bake in a preheated oven (180°C/350°F/160°C Fan/Gas 4) for about 45 minutes.

Set aside to cool.

To make the icing, mix together the icing ingredients and spread over the cold cake.

Secret
- Expect this cake to be fairly dense. The raw mixture is quite stiff so that it holds the walnuts and carrots in place and prevents them from sinking.

APPLE DAIRY-FREE FRUIT LOAF

Even though this cake has no dairy or sugar, it is still delicious – moist and full of fruit. Do not line the loaf tin with baking parchment as the cake will stick to it, just grease with butter. It freezes well.

- Cuts into 6–8 slices

> 75 g (3 oz) dried stoned prunes, roughly chopped
> 150 ml (¼ pint) boiling water
> 100 g (4 oz) self-raising flour
> ½ tsp baking powder
> ½ tsp mixed spice
> 75 g (3 oz) dried apple, chopped into large pieces
> 75 g (3 oz) dried apricots, chopped into large pieces
> 50 g (2 oz) dried pears, chopped into large pieces
> 50 g (2 oz) sultanas
> 3 tbsp apple juice
> A little demerara sugar, for sprinkling

You will need a 450 g (1 lb) loaf tin, greased and lined with non-stick baking parchment.

Measure the prunes into a heat-resistant bowl. Pour over the boiling water and set aside for about an hour to plump up and cool.

Measure the remaining ingredients into a mixing bowl, stir until smooth and fold in the prunes and soaking water. Spoon into the prepared tin, level the top and sprinkle with demerara sugar. Sit the small rack inside the small roasting tin and sit the tin on top.

TWO-, THREE- AND FOUR-OVEN AGA Slide the tin onto the grid shelf on the floor of the roasting oven with the cold sheet on the second set of runners. Bake for about an hour, until golden brown and when a skewer comes out clean when inserted into the centre of the cake.

CONVENTIONAL OVEN Bake in a preheated oven (180°C/350°F/160°C Fan/Gas 4) for about 1 hour 10 minutes, until golden brown and when a skewer comes out clean when inserted into the centre of the cake.

Set aside to cool and turn out of the tin.

Secrets
- This cake is dense with fruit, so do be sure it is cooked – the skewer test is the best way to check.

- If you are unable to buy dried apples and pears, use a packet of tropical fruit medley or something similar instead.

FAT-FREE ALL BRAN LOAF

This is a very healthy cake as it has no fat and is full of fruit and fibre. The mixture is quite wet, but don't worry, this is fine. It freezes well.

• Cuts into 10 thin slices

> 50 g (2 oz) All Bran
> 75 g (3 oz) caster sugar
> 150 g (5 oz) mixed dried fruit, e.g. sultanas, currants, raisins
> 150 ml (¼ pint) skimmed or semi-skimmed milk
> 50 g (2 oz) self-raising flour

You will need a 450 g (1 lb) loaf tin, greased and lined with non-stick baking parchment.

Measure the All Bran, sugar, dried fruit and milk into a large bowl and leave to soak on the back of the Aga for about 30 minutes. Add the flour and mix with a wooden spoon until combined. Spoon into the prepared tin and level the top. Sit the small grill rack in the small Aga roasting tin, and sit the cake on top.

Two-oven Aga Slide the tin onto the grid shelf on the floor of the roasting oven with the cold sheet on the second set of runners. Bake for about 45 minutes, until golden brown and shrinking away from the sides of the tin and when a skewer comes out clean when inserted into the centre of the loaf.

Three- and four-oven Aga Slide the tin onto the grid shelf on the floor of the baking oven and bake for 50–55 minutes. Check after 30 minutes and if a perfect golden brown, slide the cold sheet onto the second set of runners and bake until shrinking away from the sides of the tin and when a skewer comes out clean when inserted into the centre of the loaf.

Conventional oven Bake in a preheated oven (160°C/325°F/140°C Fan/Gas 3) for about an hour.

Set aside to cool in the tin, remove the baking parchment and slice into thin strips, spread with a little butter, if liked.

Secrets
• Do not worry about the large strips of All Bran; once the liquid is added it goes to mush. It is not very attractive as a raw mixture but turns into a delicious cake once baked!

• When sitting the small grill rack in the roasting tin, put it in so the rack is at the bottom and the supports are facing upwards. This protects the cake from getting too brown underneath and the sides of the tin protect the sides of the cake from burning.

RASPBERRY AND ALMOND GATEAU

There is no fat in this cake so it's very light and fluffy. This gateau is four thin layers of cake, layered with yoghurt and raspberries – it is certainly impressive enough for a party celebration. It freezes well unfilled.

- Cuts into 8 wedges

  100 g (4 oz) caster sugar
  4 eggs
  100 g (4 oz) self-raising flour
  50 g (2 oz) ground almonds
  1 tsp almond extract

- For the filling and topping

  3 x 150 g pots raspberry yoghurt
  1 x 150 g pot Greek yoghurt
  450 g (1 lb) fresh raspberries
  2 tbsp raspberry jam
  1 tbsp water

You will need two 20 cm (8 in)-diameter sandwich cake tins, each greased and base lined with a disc of non-stick baking parchment.

Measure the sugar and eggs into a large bowl and whisk with an electric hand whisk until light and fluffy and when the whisk is lifted it leaves a trail in the mixture.

Sieve the flour into the egg mixture and carefully fold in. Fold in the ground almonds and almond extract and spoon into the prepared tins.

TWO-OVEN AGA Slide the tins onto the grid shelf on the floor of the roasting oven, with the cold sheet on the second set of runners. Bake for 15–20 minutes, until golden brown.

THREE- AND FOUR-OVEN AGA Slide the tins onto the grid shelf on the floor of the baking oven and bake for about 20 minutes. Watch carefully and if the gateau is getting too dark, slide the cold sheet onto the second set of runners.

CONVENTIONAL OVEN Bake in a preheated oven (180°C/350°F/160°C Fan/Gas 4) for 20–25 minutes.

Run a knife around the edge of the cakes and leave to cool in the tin. Turn out onto a wire rack and remove the baking parchment. Once completely cold, cut each cake in half horizontally using a bread knife. Mix together both yoghurts in a bowl and mix with a third of the raspberries.

Arrange one cake on a stand, spread with a quarter of the yoghurt mixture and continue layering so the top cake just has a thin layer of yoghurt on top. Melt the raspberry jam and water in a small pan until hot. Arrange the remaining raspberries in a neat pattern on top of the cake and glaze with the jam, using a pastry brush. Transfer to the fridge for the glaze to set.

Keep in the fridge until serving.

Secret
- I have used yoghurt instead of cream to keep the fat content down, but you could use whipped cream or raspberry fromage frais, if preferred.

COTTAGE GARDEN CAKE

This really is an unusual cake and, of course, with the courgettes and seeds, is good for you too – in a roundabout way! It freezes well.

- Cuts into 12 wedges

> 2 eggs
> 150 ml (5 fl oz) vegetable oil
> 150 g (5 oz) caster sugar
> 150 g (5 oz) small courgettes, coarsely grated
> 100 g (4 oz) self-raising flour
> 100 g (4 oz) wholemeal plain flour
> 2 tsp baking powder
> 2 tbsp poppy seeds
> 2 tbsp sunflower seeds

- For the icing

> 1 x 250 g tub light mascarpone cheese
> 2 tbsp icing sugar
> Poppy seeds, for decoration

You will need a 20 cm (8 in)-diameter cake tin, greased and base lined with a disc of non-stick baking parchment.

Measure the eggs, oil and sugar into a large mixing bowl and beat well with a wooden spoon. Add the remaining ingredients and beat well until combined. Spoon into the prepared tin.

TWO-OVEN AGA Slide the tin onto the grid shelf on the floor of the roasting oven with the cold sheet on the second set of runners. Bake for 35–40 minutes, until golden brown and shrinking away from the sides of the tin.

THREE- AND FOUR-OVEN AGA Slide the tin onto the grid shelf on the floor of the baking oven and bake for about 45 minutes, until golden brown and shrinking away from the sides of the tin. If the cake is getting too brown, slide the cold sheet onto the second set of runners.

CONVENTIONAL OVEN Bake in a preheated oven (180°C/350°F/160°C Fan/Gas 4) for 35–40 minutes.

Allow to cool in the tin and then, once cold, remove the baking parchment and sit on a plate.

To make the icing, mix together the mascarpone cheese and icing sugar and beat until smooth. Spread over the cold cake and sprinkle with poppy seeds for decoration.

Secret
- Use small courgettes, as large ones can be too wet, and don't peel them. It is better to keep the green skin on so that they hold their shape and you can see the colour.

DOUBLE-DECKER BLUEBERRY AND LEMON CAKE

This looks so attractive and is very quick to make – it is a fatless sponge, based on a Swiss roll recipe, but I have made it a little thicker and into a double-decker instead of rolling it. It freezes well before cutting or filling.

- Cuts into 8 generous slices

> 4 eggs
> 100 g (4 oz) caster sugar
> Finely grated rind of 1 large lemon
> 100 g (4 oz) self-raising flour

- For the filling

> 1 x pot half-fat crème fraîche
> 150 g (5 oz) fresh blueberries
> About ½ jar luxury lemon curd

You will need a small Aga roasting tin (or traybake tin measuring 30 x 23 cm/12 x 9 in). Cut a rectangle of non-stick baking parchment just larger than the base and sides of the tin. Grease the tin and then line with the baking parchment, pushing it neatly into the corners to fit.

Whisk the eggs and sugar, preferably using an electric hand whisk or tabletop electric mixer, until the mixture is light and frothy and has increased in volume. When the whisk is lifted out of the bowl, the mixture falling off it should leave a trail. Add the lemon rind and sift in the flour, carefully folding in at the same time using a metal spoon. Turn the mixture into the prepared tin, spreading it gently into the corners.

TWO-, THREE- AND FOUR-OVEN AGA Slide the tin onto the grid shelf on the floor of the roasting oven and bake for 10–12 minutes, until golden brown and shrinking away from the sides of the tin.

CONVENTIONAL OVEN Bake in a preheated oven (200°C/400°F/180°C Fan/Gas 6) for 10–12 minutes.

Place a piece of non-stick baking parchment a little bigger than the size of the tin onto a work surface. Invert the cake onto the paper and remove the baking parchment. Leave to cool.

Once cold, trim all four edges of the cake with a bread knife. Cut the cake in half lengthways. Arrange one half on a serving dish. Mix the crème fraîche with half the blueberries and stir in two-thirds of the lemon curd (no need to mix it in completely, just so it is swirled). Spread over the cake on the plate and then sit the other half on top. Spread the rest of the lemon curd over the cake and scatter with the remaining blueberries.

Secrets

- You can use whipped cream or full-fat crème fraîche instead of the half-fat crème fraîche, if preferred.

- Do not overcook or the cake will be dry.

WHOLEMEAL CRANBERRY ROCK CAKES

Rock cakes have a wonderful history as they have been around for ages and were a great favourite of many generations before us. They are not very sweet (similar to a scone, in fact), and my version is slightly healthier as I use half wholemeal flour; but use all white self-raising flour if you prefer. They freeze well.

- Makes 12 rock cakes

> 100 g (4 oz) self-raising flour
> 100 g (4 oz) wholemeal plain flour
> 2 tsp baking powder
> 100 g (4 oz) butter, softened
> 50 g (2 oz) light muscovado sugar
> 100 g (4 oz) dried cranberries, snipped in half
> 1 egg
> About 2 tbsp milk
> A little demerara sugar, for sprinkling

You will need a large Aga roasting tin or baking sheet, greased.

Measure both the flours and the baking powder into a mixing bowl. Using your hands, rub in the butter until it resembles breadcrumbs. This can be done in a processor if easier. Stir in the sugar and cranberries.

In a separate bowl, whisk together the egg and milk with a fork and pour onto the mixture, mixing with your hands until combined. If a little dry, add a touch more milk.

Using two teaspoons, spoon 12 rough mounds onto the baking sheet and sprinkle with demerara sugar.

Two-, three- and four-oven Aga Slide the tin or baking sheet onto the grid shelf on the floor of the roasting oven, with the cold sheet on the second set of runners. Bake for 10–12 minutes, until golden brown and cooked through.

Conventional oven Bake in a preheated oven (200°C/400°F/180°C Fan/Gas 6) for 12–15 minutes.

Transfer to a wire rack to cool.

Secrets
- By using half wholemeal flour, the rock cake mixture is a little drier than normal, so you may need to add a little more milk to the mixture when beating.

- You can replace the cranberries with other dried fruits, if preferred.

SEEDED FRUIT BARS

These look so attractive and feel good for you when you are eating them – perfect for after the gym! They aren't suitable for freezing.

- Makes 18 bars

> 100 g (4 oz) butter
> 100 g (4 oz) light muscovado sugar
> 75 g (3 oz) golden syrup
> 175 g (6 oz) dried fruit, e.g. apricots, peaches, apples, pears, mangoes, pineapples
> 200 g (8 oz) porridge oats
> 50 g (2 oz) pumpkin seeds
> 50 g (2 oz) sunflower seeds
> 25 g (1 oz) sesame seeds

You will need a small Aga roasting tin (or traybake tin measuring 30 x 23 cm/12 x 9 in), greased and lined with non-stick baking parchment.

Measure the butter, sugar and golden syrup into a saucepan. Heat on the simmering plate (or on the hob set to a low heat), until the butter has melted and the sugar dissolved. Cut the dried fruits into small pieces, the size of a sultana.

Measure the remaining ingredients into a mixing bowl, add the chopped dried fruit and pour over the warm butter mixture. Stir until combined and the dry ingredients are coated. Spoon into the prepared tin and level the top with the back of a spoon.

TWO-OVEN AGA Slide the tin onto the grid shelf on the floor of the roasting oven with the cold sheet on the second set of runners. Bake for 15–20 minutes, until golden brown.

THREE- AND FOUR-OVEN AGA Slide the tin onto the grid shelf on the floor of the baking oven and bake for 15–20 minutes, until golden brown.

CONVENTIONAL OVEN Bake in a preheated oven (160°C/325°F/140°C Fan/Gas 3) for 20–25 minutes.

Once removed from the oven, set aside until lukewarm, tip out onto a board and cut into six equal slices across the long side and three equal slices across the short side to give you 18 pieces. Transfer to a wire rack to cool.

Secret

- You can buy mixed dried fruit in bags – they are often called fruit medley or tropical fruit medley. I prefer to use these fruits for this recipe rather than sultanas, currants or raisins as the flavour is sweeter and the colours look lovely.

Seeded fruit bars (right) and Honey and date oat bars (left, see page 128)

HONEY AND DATE OAT BARS

These are similar to flapjacks but with added fruit and honey. They freeze well. (See the photograph on page 127.)

- Makes 24 bars

> 150 g (5 oz) butter, cut into cubes
> 75 g (3 oz) light muscovado sugar
> 3 tbsp runny honey
> 250 g (9 oz) porridge oats
> 175 g (6 oz) dried stoned dates, cut into small pieces
> 50 g (2 oz) roasted chopped hazelnuts

You will need a small Aga roasting tin (or traybake tin measuring 30 x 23 cm/12 x 9 in), greased and lined with non-stick baking parchment.

Measure the butter into a pan, add the sugar and honey and heat on the simmering plate (or on the hob set to a low heat), stirring until the butter has melted and the sugar dissolved. Remove from the heat, stir in the oats and dates.

Tip the mixture into the prepared tin and press the top with the back of a spoon until even. Sprinkle with the hazelnuts and press down slightly using your fingers.

TWO-OVEN AGA Slide the tin onto the grid shelf on the floor of the roasting oven with the cold sheet on the second set of runners. Bake for about 12 minutes, until golden brown.

THREE- AND FOUR-OVEN AGA Slide the tin onto the grid shelf on the floor of the baking oven and bake for about 15 minutes, until golden brown.

CONVENTIONAL OVEN Bake in a preheated oven (160°C/325°F/140°C Fan/Gas 3) for 20–25 minutes.

Once removed from the oven and while still warm, cut into eight equal slices across the long side and three equal slices across the short side to give you 24 pieces. Once cold, remove from the tin.

Secret
- Many people have a nut allergy, so if this is the case with your family and friends, then omit the hazelnuts and leave the top plain; it is just as delicious.

BREAKFAST MUESLI BARS

These are similar to the grain bars you can buy, but taste heaps better! They freeze well.

- Makes 24 bars

>150 g (5 oz) butter, cut into cubes
>75 g (3 oz) caster sugar
>3 tbsp golden syrup
>400 g (14 oz) fruit and nut muesli

You will need a small Aga roasting tin (or traybake tin measuring 30 x 23 cm/12 x 9 in), greased and lined with non-stick baking parchment.

Measure the butter into a large pan, add the sugar and golden syrup and heat on the simmering plate (or on the hob set to a low heat), stirring until the butter has melted and the sugar dissolved. Remove from the heat and stir in the muesli until combined. Tip into the prepared tin and press the top with the back of a spoon until even.

TWO-OVEN AGA Slide the tin onto the grid shelf on the floor of the roasting oven with the cold sheet on the second set of runners. Bake for 15–20 minutes, until golden brown.

THREE- AND FOUR-OVEN AGA Slide the tin onto the grid shelf on the floor of the baking oven and bake for 20–25 minutes, until golden brown.

CONVENTIONAL OVEN Bake in a preheated oven (160°C/325°F/140°C Fan/Gas 3) for 20–25 minutes.

Once removed from the oven and while still warm, cut into eight equal slices across the long side and three equal slices across the short side to give you 24 pieces. Once cold, remove from the tin.

Secret

- You can buy plain or fruit and nut muesli, both work just as well – if using plain muesli, use 350 g (12 oz) and add 50 g (2 oz) of dried fruit.

Traditional cakes

These traditional recipes are perfect for special occasions, as well as old English regional classics, which will be enjoyed by all family and friends. Traditional cakes often have more ingredients and longer baking methods than modern cakes, so I have brought them up-to-date with flavour and technique, making each recipe simpler to make and bake.

BOOZY FRUIT CAKE

A beautifully moist, rich cake that is perfect for Christmas or can be served plain at any time of year. It's really boozy, so there is no need to feed it with alcohol once made. Make the cake at least four weeks ahead so that it is not crumbly when cut; this gives the fruit and sponge a chance to 'set', therefore making cutting easier. Decorate with traditional icing or with glazed fruits. It freezes well un-iced.

- Cuts into 10–12 wedges

> 225 g (8 oz) butter, softened
> 225 g (8 oz) light muscovado sugar
> 225 g (8 oz) plain flour
> 4 eggs
> 90 ml (3½ fl oz) dark rum
> 225 g (8 oz) raisins
> 450 g (1 lb) sultanas
> 225 g (8 oz) dried cranberries
> 175 g (6 oz) glacé cherries, rinsed, dried and cut into quarters
> 175 g (6 oz) dried apricots, cut into raisin-sized pieces

You will need a deep, 20 cm (8 in)-diameter cake tin, greased and base lined with non-stick baking parchment.

Measure the butter and sugar into a large mixing bowl, and cream with a wooden spoon. Add the remaining ingredients and continue to mix until combined. Spoon the mixture into the prepared tin and spread out evenly with the back of a spoon.

TWO-, THREE- AND FOUR-OVEN AGA Slide the tin onto the grid shelf on the floor of the simmering oven and bake for 6–9 hours, until dark golden and when a skewer comes out clean when inserted into the centre of the cake.

CONVENTIONAL OVEN Bake in a preheated oven (140°C/275°F/120°C Fan/Gas 1) for 4–4½ hours. Check after 2 hours, and if the cake is a perfect colour, cover with foil.

Leave to cool in the tin, then remove, wrap in baking parchment and foil and store.

Secret

- Simmering ovens do vary so much, hence the time difference. Mine took 8 hours but yours may vary. This is especially the case for re-conditioned Agas as the simmering oven can be very cool. If this is the case or your Aga is very old, start the cake off on the grid shelf on the floor of the roasting oven with the cold sheet on the second set of runners and bake for about 15 minutes or until pale golden. Carefully transfer the now hot cold sheet to the simmering oven, sit the cake on top of the sheet and continue to cook as above until a skewer comes out clean when inserted into the centre of the cake.

MARY'S MALT LOAF

This recipe was mentioned to me by a friend of mine who said that she often makes it and loves it – it was only when I told Mary Berry about it that she said that it's her recipe and in her 1979 cake book! This so often happens with recipes, the original often came from Mary, the Queen of Cakes! No fat and no eggs, this is a healthy cake. It freezes well.

- Cuts into about 15 thin slices

> 225 g (8 oz) self-raising flour
> 50 g (2 oz) Ovaltine
> 50 g (2 oz) caster sugar
> 100 g (4 oz) dried mixed fruit, e.g. sultanas, currants, raisins
> 150 ml (¼ pint) skimmed or semi-skimmed milk
> 2 tbsp golden syrup
> A little demerara sugar, for sprinkling

You will need a 450 g (1 lb) loaf tin, greased and lined with non-stick baking parchment.

Measure all the ingredients into a large mixing bowl and beat well using a wooden spoon until combined. Spoon into the prepared tin, level the top and sprinkle with demerara sugar.

TWO-OVEN AGA Slide the tin onto the grid shelf on the floor of the roasting oven with the cold sheet on the second set of runners. Bake for 25–30 minutes, until golden brown and shrinking away from the sides of the tin.

THREE- AND FOUR-OVEN AGA Slide the tin onto the grid shelf on the floor of the roasting oven and bake for 35–40 minutes, until golden brown and shrinking away from the sides of the tin. If the malt loaf is getting too brown, slide the cold sheet onto the second set of runners.

CONVENTIONAL OVEN Line a traybake tin measuring 30 x 23 cm (12 x 9 in) with foil and grease. Bake in a preheated oven (180°C/350°F/160°C Fan/Gas 4) for about 30 minutes.

Set aside to cool. Once cold, remove from the tin and cut into thin slices and spread with butter, if liked.

Secret
- Malt extract is hard to buy nowadays, so the malt in the Ovaltine gives the malt flavour. You could use another malt drink if preferred, such as Horlicks or Bonnervita.

MONK'S GARDEN CHRISTMAS CAKE

Since we were young children, my lovely Ma has made this cake every year without fail. The family is so large now she often makes five, one for each household — what a star! It freezes well.

• Cuts into 20 pieces

300 g (10 oz) butter, soft
300 g (10 oz) soft muscovado sugar
6 eggs, beaten
500 g (1 lb 2 oz) currants
225 g (8 oz) sultanas
225 g (8 oz) raisins
100 g (4 oz) candied peel, chopped finely

175 g (6 oz) glacé cherries, rinsed, dried and cut into quarters
Finely grated rind of 1 lemon
300 g (10 oz) plain flour
½ tsp mixed spice
½ tsp cinnamon powder
2 tbsp milk

You will need a deep, 23 cm (9 in)-diameter cake tin, greased and lined with baking parchment.

Measure the butter and sugar into a large mixing bowl and beat with a wooden spoon until light and creamed. Gradually add the eggs, beating with a wooden spoon between each addition. Stir in the fruit, candied peel, cherries and lemon rind. Then stir in the flour, spice and cinnamon. Add a little milk until the mixture is soft enough to drop from a spoon. Spoon into the prepared tin and level the top.

TWO-, THREE- AND FOUR-OVEN AGA Slide the tin into the simmering oven and bake for 7–10 hours, until a skewer comes out clean when inserted into the centre of the cake.

CONVENTIONAL OVEN Line the tin with a double layer of baking parchment. Bake in a preheated oven (160°C/325°F/140°C Fan/Gas 3) for about 4 hours. Check after about 2 hours and, if the cake is getting too brown, cover it with foil or baking parchment.

Leave to cool in the tin, then remove from the tin, wrap in baking parchment and foil and keep in a cool place. Once a week turn the cake upside down and skewer through the cake at regular intervals. Pour brandy into the skewer holes — just enough to soak in. Do this as much or as little as you like until Christmas!

Secrets

• Because of the amount of fruit in a Christmas cake, a fresh cake may crumble when cut therefore it is best made a minimum of six weeks ahead (maximum of six months).

• Be sure to store it in a cool place, well wrapped, in baking parchment and foil. If kept in a warm kitchen near the Aga, the cake could go mouldy.

• The baking time varies greatly in an Aga, so if you are short of time, make the raw cake mixture and put it into the tin, cover with cling film and keep in the larder. Bake the next day when you have time to check the timings.

CHRISTMAS CAKE DECORATION

Marzipan

You can buy marzipan easily from good supermarkets, but if you would like to make your own, here is a simple recipe. Marzipan is the modern word for traditional almond paste – they are the same thing. This recipe makes enough to cover a 23 cm (9 in)-diameter cake.

- Makes about 675 g (1½ lb)

> 225 g (8 oz) ground almonds
> 225 g (8 oz) caster sugar
> 225 g (8 oz) icing sugar, sifted
> 4 egg yolks, or 2 whole eggs
> About 6 drops almond extract

Mix together the ground almonds and sugars in a bowl, add the yolks or whole eggs and almond extract. Mix until combined, tip onto the worktop and knead together to form a stiff paste. Do not over-knead as this will make the paste oily. Wrap in cling film and store in the fridge until required.

- TO COVER A CAKE WITH MARZIPAN

This is a basic description of how to cover a cake for Christmas or for a wedding. You will need apricot glaze to stick the marzipan to the cake and to keep the moisture in the cake. Heat about four tablespoons of apricot jam with a tablespoon of water or lemon juice, until melted.

Stand the cake on a cake board that is 5 cm (2 in) larger than the size of the cake. Brush the cake all over with a little apricot glaze.

Lightly dust a work surface with sifted icing sugar and then roll out the marzipan to about 4 cm (1¾ in) larger than the top and sides of the cake. Carefully lift the marzipan over the cake with the help of a rolling pin. Gently level and smooth the marzipan over the top and down the sides. Use a rolling pin to ensure the top and sides are flat. Neatly trim the marzipan from around the base.

- ROYAL ICING

I remember all the Christmases over the years as a child, making this icing with my mother. We all took it in turns to beat the icing as it takes a little while for it to become stiff. This icing is enough to cover a 23 cm (9 in)-diameter cake. Glycerine can be bought from pharmacies.

> 3 egg whites
> 675 g (1½ lb) icing sugar
> 3 tsp lemon juice
> 1½ tsp glycerine

Whisk the egg whites in a large bowl until they become frothy but not stiff. Sieve in the icing sugar, a spoonful at a time, and fold in. Stir in the lemon juice and glycerine. Beat the icing for a few minutes until it is very stiff and white and stands up in peaks.

Set the icing aside until needed, covered with a damp tea towel. Just before icing, give it one more beat with a wooden spoon and, using a palette knife, spread the icing over the cake to give a smooth finish, or cover the cake with the icing and spike it into peaks for a rough icing.

INGREDIENT QUANTITIES DEPENDING ON THE SIZE OF YOUR CAKE TIN

	18 cm (7 in) round / 15 cm (6 in) square	20 cm (8 in) round / 18 cm (7 in) square	23 cm (9 in) round / 20 cm (8 in) square	25 cm (10 in) round / 23 cm (9 in) square	28cm (11 in) round / 25cm (10 in) square	30cm (12 in) round / 28cm (11 in) square	33cm (13 in) round / 30cm (12 in) square
BUTTER	175 g (6 oz)	225 g (8 oz)	300 g (10 oz)	400 g (14 oz)	500 g (1 lb 2 oz)	600 g (1 lb 4 oz)	700 g (1 lb 8 oz)
SUGAR	175 g (6 oz)	225 g (8 oz)	300 g (10 oz)	400 g (14 oz)	500 g (1 lb 2 oz)	600 g (1 lb 4 oz)	700 g (1 lb 8 oz)
EGGS	4	5	6	7	8	9	10
CURRANTS	250 g (9 oz)	350 g (12 oz)	500 g (1 lb 2 oz)	600 g (1 lb 4 oz)	750 g (1 lb 9 oz)	900 g (2 lb)	1.1 kg (2 lb 7 oz)
SULTANAS	100 g (4 oz)	175 g (6 oz)	225 g (8 oz)	300 g (10 oz)	350 g (12 oz)	450 g (15 oz)	500 g (1 lb 2 oz)
RAISINS	100 g (4 oz)	175 g (6 oz)	225 g (8 oz)	300 g (10 oz)	350 g (12 oz)	450 g (15 oz)	500 g (1 lb 2 oz)
CANDIED PEEL	50 g (2 oz)	75 g (3 oz)	100 g (4 oz)	150 g (5 oz)	175 g (6 oz)	200 g (7 oz)	225 g (8 oz)
CHERRIES	100 g (4 oz)	150 g (5 oz)	175 g (6 oz)	225 g (8 oz)	300 g (10 oz)	350 g (12 oz)	400 g (14 oz)
LEMON RIND	$1/2$	$1/2$	1	1	$1\,1/2$	2	2
PLAIN FLOUR	175 g (6 oz)	225 g (8 oz)	300 g (10 oz)	400 g (14 oz)	500 g (1 lb 2 oz)	600 g (1 lb 4 oz)	700 g (1 lb 8 oz)
MIXED SPICE	$1/2$ tsp	$1/2$ tsp	$1/2$ tsp	1 tsp	$1\,1/2$ tsp	2 tsp	2 tsp
CINNAMON	$1/2$ tsp	$1/2$ tsp	$1/2$ tsp	1 tsp	$1\,1/2$ tsp	2 tsp	2 tsp
MILK	1 tbsp	1 tbsp	2 tbsp	2 tbsp	2–3 tbsp	3 tbsp	3 tbsp

CHRISTMAS YULE LOG

I think it is so nice to give an alternative to the traditional Christmas cake so this is a very easy yule log with rich, delicious frosted icing. It freezes well rolled and filled – ice up to 48 hours ahead.

- Cuts into 12–14 slices

- For the chocolate sponge

  > 6 large eggs
  > 165 g (6 oz) caster sugar
  > 90 g (3½ oz) self-raising flour
  > 65 g (2½ oz) cocoa powder

- For the chocolate frosting

  > 300 g (10 oz) icing sugar, plus extra for dusting
  > 75 g (3 oz) cocoa powder
  > 115 g (4½ oz) butter
  > 150 ml (¼ pint) water
  > 175 g (6 oz) caster sugar
  >
  > 300 ml (½ pint) double cream, whipped

You will need a large Aga roasting tin (or Swiss roll tin measuring 33 x 23 cm/12 x 9 in) together with a piping bag and star nozzle. Cut a rectangle of non-stick baking parchment just larger than the base and sides of the tin. Grease the tin and then line with the baking parchment, pushing it neatly into the corners to fit.

Whisk the eggs and sugar using an electric hand whisk in a large bowl until the mixture is pale in colour, light and frothy. The mixture should leave a trail behind when the whisk is lifted. Sift the flour and cocoa powder into the bowl and carefully fold together, using a metal spoon, until all the cocoa powder and flour are incorporated into the egg mixture. Pour into the lined tin and spread out into the corners.

TWO-, THREE- AND FOUR-OVEN AGA Slide the tin onto the grid shelf on the floor of the roasting oven. Bake for 10–12 minutes, until golden brown, shrinking away from the sides of the tin and springy to the touch. Watch carefully, if the cake gets too dark, slide the cold sheet onto the second set of runners.

CONVENTIONAL OVEN Bake in the middle of a preheated oven (220°C/425°/200°C Fan/ Gas 7) for 10–12 minutes.

Place a piece of non-stick baking parchment a little bigger than the tin onto a work surface and sprinkle it with caster sugar. While still warm, invert the cake onto the sugared paper. Quickly loosen the baking parchment on the bottom of the cake and peel it away. Using a sharp knife, score a mark 2 cm (¾ in) in from one shorter edge, being careful not to cut right through. Roll up the cake firmly with the baking parchment inside. Work from the shorter, cut end, tucking in the scored piece of sponge tightly to make a roll. Leave to cool.

To make the icing, sieve the icing sugar and cocoa powder into a large bowl. Measure the butter, water and sugar into a small saucepan. Bring to the boil on the boiling plate for 30 seconds and then pour into the icing sugar bowl and beat with a wooden spoon until smooth and glossy.

Once the Swiss roll is cold, carefully unroll the cake and spread about two tablespoons of the icing over the surface. Spread the whipped cream on top of the icing and re-roll tightly and in the same way you rolled it to begin with, using the baking parchment to guide you. Cut off a third of the cake from one end on the diagonal. Arrange the large piece of cake on a serving plate and angle the cut end to the side of the large cake to make a branch.

Fit the piping bag with the star nozzle and fill with the remaining chocolate icing. Pipe long thin lines along the cake, covering it completely so that it looks like the bark of a tree. Cover the ends of each branch with icing too.

Dust with icing sugar and decorate with freshly picked holly and serve.

Secrets

- I always used to secure the corners of the paper with paper clips, to give straight sides when lining a tin for a Swiss roll or roulade, but there is no need to do this because as long as you cut the corners to the right size, the baking parchment will sit neatly in the tin.

- When laying the baking parchment on the worktop before inverting the cake, be sure that it is wide and long enough so you have enough baking parchment to roll around the cake.

QUICK PINEAPPLE FRUIT CAKE

This is a very moist fruit cake because of the pineapple, but store it in the fridge as it could go mouldy in a cake tin. This is my version of a classic boiled fruit cake, old-fashioned but a great flavour.

- Cuts into 8 wedges

> 225 g (8 oz) caster sugar
> 1 x 425 g can crushed pineapple, drained well
> 450 g (1 lb) mixed dried fruit, e.g. sultanas, currants, cherries
> 1 tsp bicarbonate of soda
> Finely grated rind of 1 lemon
> 100 g (4 oz) butter
> 225 g (8 oz) self-raising flour
> 2 eggs

You will need a deep, 20 cm (8 in)-diameter, loose-bottomed cake tin, greased and base lined with a disc of non-stick baking parchment.

Measure the sugar, pineapple, dried fruit, bicarbonate of soda, lemon rind and butter into a saucepan and gently heat on the simmering plate (or on the hob set to a low heat), stirring until the butter has melted. Bring to the boil and boil for about 3 minutes. Remove from the heat, and set aside to cool.

Measure the flour into a large mixing bowl and pour in the cooled fruit mixture and stir well. Add the eggs and stir until completely combined. Spoon into the prepared tin and level the top.

TWO-, THREE- AND FOUR-OVEN AGA Slide the tin onto the grid shelf on the floor of the roasting oven with the cold sheet on the second set of runners. Bake for about 20 minutes, until golden brown. Transfer the now hot cold sheet into the simmering oven and sit the cake on top. Cook for about a further 2 hours, until cooked through – when a skewer inserted into the centre of the cake comes out clean.

CONVENTIONAL OVEN Bake in a preheated oven (180°C/350°F/160°C Fan/Gas 4) for about 60 minutes. You may need to cover the cake with foil halfway through if it is getting too brown.

Leave to cool in the tin.

Secret

- It is important to drain the pineapple well otherwise the excess moisture will make the fruit sink to the bottom of the cake.

SIMNEL CAKE

This has become the traditional Easter cake, but originally it was given to servant girls to take home to their mothers for Mother's Day. It keeps well; before decorating, wrap it in baking parchment and foil and store in the fridge for up to six weeks. It freezes well, too.

- Cuts into 10 wedges

> 175 g (6 oz) light muscovado sugar
> 175 g (6 oz) butter, soft
> 175 g (6 oz) self-raising flour
> 3 large eggs
> 25 g (1 oz) ground almonds
> 2 tbsp milk
> 100 g (4 oz) sultanas
> 100 g (4 oz) cherries, quartered, washed and dried
> 100 g (4 oz) dried apricots, snipped into small pieces
> 100 g (4 oz) dried cranberries, cut in half
> Finely grated rind of 1 lemon
> 2 teaspoons mixed spice
>
> 450 g (1 lb) marzipan (see page 136)
> 3 tbsp apricot jam
> 1 egg, beaten

You will need a deep, 20 cm (8 in)-diameter cake tin, greased and base lined with a disc of non-stick baking parchment.

Measure all the cake ingredients into a large mixing bowl and beat well with a wooden spoon until combined. Spoon half the mixture into the prepared tin and level the surface.

Take one-third of the marzipan and roll out to a circle the same size as the cake tin; place the circle on top of the cake mixture. Spoon the remaining mixture on top of the marzipan and level the surface.

Two-, THREE- AND FOUR-OVEN AGA – slow baking. Slide the tin onto the grid shelf in the simmering oven. Bake for 5–8 hours, until dark golden brown and a skewer comes out clean when inserted into the centre of the cake.

THREE- AND FOUR-OVEN AGA – fast baking. Slide the tin onto the grid shelf on the floor of the baking oven and bake for about 1¾ hours, turning once. If the cake is getting too brown, slide the cold sheet onto the second set of runners and protect the cake's top with a piece of baking parchment.

CONVENTIONAL OVEN Bake in a preheated oven (160°C/325°F/140°C Fan/Gas 3) for 1½–2 hours, until golden brown and firm in the middle. If, towards the end of the cooking time, the cake is getting too brown, loosely cover it with a piece of foil.

Allow the cake to cool in the tin before turning onto a wire rack. When the cake is cool, brush the top with a little warmed apricot jam. Roll out half the remaining marzipan to the size of the cake and sit it on the top. Crimp the edges of the marzipan and make a lattice pattern in the centre of the marzipan using a sharp knife.

Make 11 evenly sized balls from the remaining marzipan and arrange around the edge, pressing down so they stay in place. Brush the tops of the balls and the crimped marzipan with beaten egg. Bake at the very top of the roasting oven for about 6 minutes, until the marzipan and balls are singed golden brown. (If using a conventional oven, slide the cake under a hot grill for about 5 minutes, turning the cake round so the marzipan is evenly tinged brown all over.)

Decorate with fresh spring flowers.

Secrets

- If you have a blowtorch, you can use this to tinge the marzipan instead.

- Decorate at Easter with bunnies and chickens and for Mother's Day with fresh spring flowers in season, such as primroses and narcissi.

SPICED PARKIN

Parkin is a ginger cake with flour, oatmeal and black treacle. It originates from the north of England and was traditionally eaten on bonfire night, but now, of course, is also enjoyed all year round. It is very rich, so only serve small slices. It isn't suitable for freezing.

- Cuts into 8–10 pieces

>   100 g (4 oz) plain flour
>   225 g (8 oz) porridge oats
>   1 tsp ground ginger
>   ½ tsp mixed spice
>   ½ tsp bicarbonate of soda
>   100 g (4 oz) golden syrup
>   100 g (4 oz) black treacle
>   100 g (4 oz) butter
>   100 g (4 oz) light muscovado sugar
>   1 egg, beaten with 100 ml (3½ fl oz) milk

You will need a deep, 20 cm (8 in)-diameter cake tin, greased and base lined with a disc of non-stick baking parchment.

Measure the flour, porridge oats, ginger, spice and bicarbonate of soda into a mixing bowl.

Measure the golden syrup, treacle, butter and sugar into a pan, and gently heat on the simmering plate (or on the hob set to a low heat), stirring until smooth and blended. Pour into the dry ingredients in the mixing bowl and mix well. Add the egg and milk and beat again until smooth. Pour into the prepared tin.

TWO-, THREE- AND FOUR-OVEN AGA Slide the tin onto the grid shelf on the floor of the roasting oven, with the cold sheet on the second set of runners. Bake for about 30 minutes, until dark and with a slight crust on top. Transfer the now hot cold sheet to the simmering oven and sit the cake on top and continue to bake for a further 25 minutes, until firm in the centre and slightly shrinking away from the sides of the tin.

CONVENTIONAL OVEN Bake in a preheated oven (160°C/325°F/140°C Fan/Gas 3) for 40–50 minutes.

Leave to cool in the tin and then turn out. Remove the baking parchment and cut into pieces.

Secrets
- Don't expect the raw mixture to be thick; it will, in fact, be quite runny when pouring into the tin.

- Use traditional porridge oats for this recipe, not the jumbo oats, as they are too big.

CHOCOLATE ROULADE

Chocolate roulade is always popular at tea time or as a dessert. For a really impressive dessert to serve to many people, make four roulades and arrange them end to end on a long plank of wood, covered with foil. Dusted with icing sugar, it looks stunning. As a variation, mix a few fresh raspberries or strawberries in with the cream. It freezes well filled and rolled.

- Makes 1 roulade, cuts into 8 slices

    175 g (6 oz) dark chocolate,
      broken into pieces
    175 g (6 oz) caster sugar
    6 eggs, separated
    2 level tbsp cocoa powder, sifted

- For the filling

    300 ml (10 fl oz) double cream
    2 tsp vanilla extract
    Icing sugar

You will need a Swiss roll tin measuring 33 x 23 cm (13 x 9 in). Cut a rectangle of non-stick baking parchment just larger than the base and sides of the tin. Grease the tin and then line with the baking parchment, pushing it neatly into the corners to fit.

Break the chocolate into a bowl and sit on the back of the Aga until melted, stirring occasionally. (For a conventional oven, put the chocolate into a bowl and heat gently over a pan of simmering water, stirring until melted.) Allow to cool slightly.

Measure the sugar and egg yolks into a bowl and whisk with an electric hand whisk on a high speed until light and creamy. Add the cooled melted chocolate and stir until evenly blended.

Whisk the egg whites in a large mixing bowl until stiff but not dry. Stir a large spoonful of the egg whites into the chocolate mixture, mix gently and then fold in the remaining egg whites, then add the sifted cocoa powder. Turn into the prepared tin and gently level the surface.

TWO-, THREE- AND FOUR-OVEN AGA Slide the tin onto the grid shelf on the floor of the roasting oven, with the cold sheet on the second set of runners. Bake for 15–20 minutes, until risen and shrinking away from the baking parchment.

CONVENTIONAL OVEN Bake in a preheated oven (180°C/350°F/160°C Fan/Gas 4) for about 20 minutes.

Leave to cool in the tin – don't worry, it will sink slightly.

Whip the cream until it just holds its shape and stir in the vanilla extract. Dust a large piece of non-stick baking parchment with icing sugar. Invert the cold roulade onto the paper and peel off the baking parchment. Spread the cream over the cold roulade and, starting from one short edge, roll tightly using the baking parchment to help. Don't worry if it cracks – that is quite normal! Dust with icing sugar and cut into slices.

Secret

- Traditionally, once a roulade was baked, it was covered with a damp tea towel and left for several hours, if not overnight, to prevent from drying out. Nowadays, there is no need to do this because as long as the roulade is filled and rolled once cold, it will stay moist.

DOUBLE GINGER GINGERBREAD

Gingerbread is wonderful as a cake or a dessert. It freezes well un-iced.

- Cuts into 16 pieces

> 100 g (4 oz) butter
> 3 tbsp golden syrup
> 75 g (3 oz) dark muscovado sugar
> 200 ml (7 fl oz) apple juice
> 3 eggs
> 350 g (12 oz) plain flour
> 1 level tsp bicarbonate of soda
> 2 level tsp ground ginger
> 75 g (3 oz) stem ginger bulbs, cut into raisin-sized pieces

- For the icing

> 100 g (4 oz) icing sugar
> 5 tbsp ginger syrup from the jar
> 2 bulbs ginger, cut into raisin-sized pieces

You will need a small Aga roasting tin (or roasting tin measuring about 30 x 23 cm/ 12 x 9 in), lined with foil and greased.

Measure the butter, golden syrup and sugar into a pan and heat gently on the simmering plate (or on the hob set to a low heat). Stir until the butter has melted and the sugar dissolved. Pour in the apple juice and set aside to cool a little.

Break the eggs into a bowl and beat with a fork. Then add the remaining ingredients and the melted ingredients, and beat until smooth. Pour into the prepared tin and level the top.

Two-oven Aga Slide the tin onto the grid shelf on the floor of the roasting oven with the cold sheet on the second set of runners. Bake for 20–25 minutes, until dark golden and well risen.

Three- and four-oven Aga Slide the tin onto the grid shelf on the floor of the baking oven and bake for 25–30 minutes, until dark golden and well risen. If the gingerbread is getting too brown, slide the cold sheet onto the second set of runners.

Conventional oven Bake in a preheated oven (180°C/350°F/160°C Fan/Gas 4) for 30–35 minutes.

Once cool, remove from the tin.

For the icing, mix together the icing sugar and ginger syrup and spread over the top of the cold cake. Scatter the ginger pieces over the icing.

Secrets

- The ginger syrup is from the jar with the stem ginger bulbs in.

- This cake is extremely light and you may see the air bubbles in the sponge once baked.

LEMON MADEIRA CAKE

This is a classic cake – it is dense in texture and is served plain with no icing. I have added ground almonds to keep the texture moist. It freezes well.

- Cuts into 8 wedges

>   175 g (6 oz) butter, soft
>   175 g (6 oz) caster sugar
>   225 g (8 oz) self-raising flour
>   3 eggs
>   50 g (2 oz) ground almonds
>   Finely grated rind of 1 large lemon

You will need a deep, 20 cm (8 in)-diameter cake tin, greased and base lined with a disc of non-stick baking parchment.

Measure all the ingredients into a large mixing bowl and beat with a wooden spoon until smooth. Spoon into the prepared tin and level the top.

TWO-OVEN AGA Slide the tin onto the grid shelf on the floor of the roasting oven with the cold sheet on the second set of runners. Bake for about 40 minutes, until golden brown and when a skewer comes out clean when inserted into the centre of the cake.

THREE- AND FOUR-OVEN AGA Slide the tin onto the grid shelf on the floor of the baking oven and bake for about 45 minutes, until golden brown and when a skewer comes out clean when inserted into the centre of the cake. Check after 30 minutes and if the cake is getting too brown, slide the cold sheet onto the second set of runners.

CONVENTIONAL OVEN Bake in a preheated oven (180°C/350°F/160°C Fan/Gas 4) for about an hour.

Leave in the tin to cool, remove the baking parchment and cut into wedges.

Secret

- You can also make this cake in a freestanding mixer or a processor – be careful not to over-whiz otherwise the cake will be flat.

EARL GREY TEABREAD

Teabread is a traditional cake and is making a comeback. This is my variation, using Earl Grey, which gives a lovely lemony flavour. Teabread is known in Wales as barabrith, barm brack in Ireland and Selkirk bannock in Scotland. You need to start this teabread the day before as the dried fruits need soaking in hot tea overnight to give them time to swell. It freezes well.

* Makes 2 x 450 g (1 lb) loaves, each of which cuts into 12 slices

> 350 g (12 oz) mixed dried fruit, e.g. sultanas, raisins, currants, cherries
> 225 g (8 oz) light muscovado sugar
> 300 ml (10 fl oz) hot Earl Grey tea, using two tea bags
> 300 g (10 oz) self-raising flour
> finely grated rind of 1 lemon
> 1 egg, beaten

You will need two 450 g (1 lb) loaf tins, each greased and lined with non-stick baking parchment.

The night before, measure the mixed dried fruit and sugar into a medium bowl, stir to mix, then pour the hot tea over the fruit. Cover the bowl with a tea towel or cling film and leave in a cool place overnight to allow the fruits to plump up.

Add the flour, lemon rind and beaten egg to the fruit mixture and stir with a wooden spoon until thoroughly mixed. Spoon into the prepared tins and level the surface. Sit the two tins in the large Aga roasting tin.

TWO-OVEN AGA Slide the tins onto the grid shelf on the floor of the roasting oven with the cold sheet on the second set of runners. Bake for about 35 minutes, until golden brown. Transfer the tins (still standing in the roasting tin) to the simmering oven and continue to bake for a further 45 minutes, until a skewer comes out clean when inserted into the centre of the cakes.

THREE- AND FOUR-OVEN AGA Slide the tins (no need for the roasting tin) onto the grid shelf on the floor of the baking oven and bake for about 40 minutes, until golden brown. Slide the cold sheet onto the second set of runners and continue to bake for a further 20 minutes, until a skewer comes out clean when inserted into the centre of the cake.

CONVENTIONAL OVEN Bake in a preheated oven (150°C/300°F/130°C Fan/Gas 2) for about 1½ hours. There is no need to sit the tins in a roasting tin, just slide them straight into the oven.

Allow to cool a little in the tin, then turn out and remove the baking parchment. Serve the teabread sliced and buttered.

Secret
* Sitting the loaf tins in the roasting tin prevents the base and sides of the cake from getting too brown before the centre is cooked. You can, of course, use regular tea if you prefer it to Earl Grey.

AGA BRANDY SNAPS

These are my father's favourite snack; he breaks bits off and eats them like biscuits
– very naughty! They can be a little tricky to make as they can burn very easily because
of the high sugar content, but if you are worried, see my cheat's secret, below! You can
only bake four at a time, so will need to bake in batches. They freeze well.

- Makes 24 brandy snaps

50 g (2 oz) butter	50 g (2 oz) plain flour
50 g (2 oz) demerara sugar	½ tsp ground ginger
50 g (2 oz) golden syrup	½ tsp lemon juice

You will need a baking sheet, greased and lined with non-stick baking parchment.

Measure the butter, sugar and golden syrup into a pan and gently heat on the simmering plate
(or on the hob set to a low heat), stirring until the sugar has dissolved. Set aside to cool slightly.

Sieve the flour and ginger into the mixture and stir well until combined. Spoon teaspoonfuls
of the mixture onto the baking sheets about 10 cm (4 in) apart as they spread a lot – you will
probably get only about four on each tray.

TWO-OVEN AGA Slide the baking sheet onto the grid shelf on the floor of the roasting
oven, with the cold sheet on the second set of runners. Bake for 6–8 minutes, until the
brandy snaps have spread into a circle and are dark golden brown.

THREE- AND FOUR-OVEN AGA Slide the baking sheet onto the grid shelf on the floor of
the baking oven and bake for about 8 minutes. If the snaps are getting too brown, slide the
cold sheet onto the second set of runners.

CONVENTIONAL OVEN Bake in a preheated oven (160°C/325°F/140°C Fan/Gas 3) for
about 8 minutes.

Set aside, until just cool enough to handle and shape as desired. For cigar shapes, mould
around the handle of an oiled wooden spoon. For round nests, shape over an oiled teacup
or fresh orange. For square nest boxes, shape round a small packet of butter, wrapped in
cling film – you can have fun with lots of different shapes.

Once cold, fill with a variety of fillings, such as whipped cream, ice cream, yoghurt, crème
fraîche and fromage frais, all with fresh fruits and serve.

Secrets

- It is important to mould the brandy snaps while they are still warm otherwise they set flat
  and become too brittle to mould.

- To cheat, buy brandy snaps, arrange on a baking sheet and transfer to the simmering oven for
  about 5 minutes, just enough time for them to un-curl and become flat. You can then re-
  shape them into the shape of your choice – and they will look very homemade! You can also do
  this, if you are not happy with your original shape and want to mould them again.

BUTTERMILK SULTANA SCONES

These scones are quite creamy because of the addition of the buttermilk, but they are not very sweet, as are most scones served with jam, so the buttermilk will add to the sweetness. They freeze well. (See the photograph on page 153.)

- Makes 10 scones

  225 g (8 oz) self-raising flour
  2 tsp baking powder
  50 g (2 oz) caster sugar
  40 g (1½ oz) butter, softened
  100 ml (3½ fl oz) buttermilk, plus a little extra for glazing
  1 egg, beaten
  50 g (2 oz) sultanas

- To serve

  Clotted cream
  Strawberry jam

- To serve

  Whipped or clotted cream
  Strawberry jam

You will need a baking sheet, greased, and a 4 cm (2 in) fluted scone cutter.

Measure the flour, baking powder, sugar and butter into a freestanding mixer or processor and mix until like breadcrumbs. Measure the buttermilk into a measuring jug, add the egg and beat with a fork to mix. Start the processor and gradually pour in the milk and egg and whiz until combined.

Remove the dough onto a floured work surface. Knead in the sultanas until a smooth dough has formed. Roll with a rolling pin to about 1 cm (½ in) thick. Using a scone cutter, cut out the scones, re-rolling the dough until all is used.

Arrange on the prepared baking sheet and brush the top of each scone with a little more buttermilk.

Two-, three- and four-oven Aga Slide the baking sheet onto the grid shelf on the floor of the roasting oven and bake for 12–15 minutes, until well risen and golden brown.

Conventional oven Bake in a preheated oven (200°C/400°F/180°C Fan/Gas 6) for 10–12 minutes.

Transfer to a wire rack to cool. Once cold, break in half and top with whipped or clotted cream and strawberry jam.

Secrets

- Buttermilk can be found near the regular creams in the supermarkets' chilled cabinets.

- The correct way to eat a scone is to break the scone in half with your fingers, do not cut with a knife!

MINI SCONES

Children love making scones as they are easy to mix and the kneading is great fun! These scones are small and perfect for serving when people are eating standing up, as they just pop in the mouth in one go! I made them for my youngest niece's christening and they were a big hit. They freeze well.

- Makes 22 mini scones

> 225 g (8 oz) self-raising flour
> 2 tsp baking powder
> 40 g (1½ oz) butter, softened
> 25 g (1 oz) caster sugar
> 1 egg
> About 150 ml (¼ pint) milk

You will need a baking sheet, greased, and a 2 cm (1 in) fluted scone cutter.

Measure the flour, baking powder, sugar and butter into a freestanding mixer or processor and mix until like breadcrumbs. Break the egg into a measuring jug, beat with a fork and pour in enough milk to make to just over 150 ml (¼ pint), beat again to mix. Start the processor and gradually pour in the milk and egg, leaving about a tablespoon in the jug for glazing. Whiz until combined – it's better to have a slightly sticky mixture.

Remove the dough and knead on a floured work surface until a smooth dough has formed. Roll with a rolling pin to about 1 cm (½ in) thick. Using a scone cutter, cut out the scones, re-rolling the dough until all is used.

Arrange on the prepared baking sheet and brush the top of each scone with the remaining egg and milk mixture.

TWO-, THREE- AND FOUR-OVEN AGA Slide the baking sheet onto the floor of the roasting oven and bake for 9–11 minutes, until well risen and golden brown.

CONVENTIONAL OVEN Bake in a preheated oven (200°C/400°F/180°C Fan/Gas 6) for 10–12 minutes.

Transfer to a wire rack to cool. Once cold, break in half and top with clotted cream and strawberry jam.

Secrets

- When cutting out the scones with a scone cutter, do not twist the cutter otherwise the scone will not rise evenly.

- There is a debate with scones as to whether the jam or the cream goes on first and I think it depends which part of the West Country you come from – I think in Devon and Cornwall they serve them differently. Personally, I put the jam on first and then top with a dollop of cream. I do not butter my scones as I think both cream and butter is a bit much!

Mini scones (front) and Buttermilk sultana scones (back, see page 151).

T E E N Y - W E E N Y   M E R I N G U E S

Serving meringues for tea is really smart and quite old fashioned — the top hotels still serve meringues as a cream tea and I think it's enchanting. Cooked meringues will keep wrapped in a bag in a cool place for up to two months. They freeze well, but can be easily crushed, so freeze in a box.

- Makes about 30 meringues

      4 egg whites
      225 g (8 oz) caster sugar

- For the filling

      150 ml (¼ pint) double cream, whipped
      fresh raspberries or strawberries

You will need a baking sheet, greased and lined with non-stick baking parchment, and a piping bag and 5 mm (¼ in) plain nozzle.

Put the egg whites into a large bowl (or the bowl of a freestanding mixer). Whisk with an electric hand whisk on high speed until white and fluffy, like a cloud. Still whisking on maximum speed, gradually add the sugar, a teaspoon at a time, until incorporated and the meringue is stiff and shiny and stands upright on the whisk.

Spoon the meringue into the piping bag fitted with the nozzle and pipe a very small (about the size of a £2 coin) circle. Then pipe again around the edge of the circle in one layer — this will give a little nest. Continue piping the nests until you have used all the meringue. If you are not keen on piping, spoon teaspoonfuls onto the baking parchment and use the back of the spoon to make an indent in the centre of each meringue.

T W O -, T H R E E - A N D F O U R - O V E N A G A Put the baking sheet anywhere in the simmering oven and bake for about 50 minutes, until the meringues are just firm to the touch and can be easily removed from the baking parchment.

C O N V E N T I O N A L O V E N Bake in a preheated oven (140°C/275°F/120°C Fan/Gas 1) for about 45 minutes.

Remove the meringues from the baking parchment onto a wire rack and set aside until stone cold. Spoon a little cream into the centre of each nest and top with a raspberry or quarter strawberry. Keep in the fridge until ready to serve.

Secrets
There are lots of meringue tips!

- Make sure there is no egg yolk in the egg whites otherwise they will not whisk successfully.

- The eggs can be from the fridge, at room temperature and a few days old or fresh — it makes no difference! They may just whisk up a bit quicker if at room temperature.

- Use a freestanding mixer, e.g. KitchenAid or Kenwood or an electric hand whisk in a large bowl – this will take longer to make (up to about 10 minutes) as the whisks are smaller than on a machine.

- Do not use a machine with a lid on it – the idea is to get air into the egg whites.

- Do not add the sugar too soon otherwise the air will be knocked out of the egg whites. Instead, add it once the whites are as stiff as they can get and then add the sugar gradually, still whisking hard. This is the secret as the sugar will then stay suspended in the whites.

- To fill a piping bag, roll down the sides of the bag (as you would when putting your stockings on!), then fill it or sit it in a jug and it will be easier to fill and won't go everywhere. As it fills up, just roll the sides up higher.

- If the meringues do not come off the paper easily after 50 minutes, it means they are not completely cooked, so return to the oven until they easily come off the paper.

USEFUL ADDRESSES

Aga Rayburn

Station Road
Ketley, Telford, Shropshire TF1 5AQ
Head office: 01952 642000
Cookware enquiries: 01952 642111
Aga care service line: 0845 6023015
Technical service helpline:
　　01952 642060
www.aga-web.co.uk
www.agalinks.com

ICTC

3 Caley Close
Sweet Briar Road
Norwich, Norfolk NR3 2BU
Tel: 01603 488019
www.ictc.co.uk
(Equipment manufacturer)

KitchenAid

c/o Maytag UK
2 St Annes's Boulevard
Foxboro Business Park
Redhill, Surrey RH1 1AX
Consumer helpline: 0080038104026
www.kitchenaid.co.uk
(Makers of the iconic stand mixer)

Lakeland

Alexandra Buildings
Windemere, Cumbria LA23 1BQ
Tel: 01539 488100
www.lakeland.co.uk
(Cookware and specialised equipment)

Magimix UK Ltd

19 Bridge Street
Godalming, Surrey GU7 1HY
Tel: 01483 427411 (1)
www.magimix.com
(Equipment manufacturer)

Lucy Young is the new young Aga talent. She has a *Cordon Bleu* training and has worked with Mary Berry for over 17 years, helping create and test Mary's recipes for books and TV and teaching at her very popular Aga workshops. Lucy has often appeared on the UKTV Food Channel and is regularly interviewed on radio. She is the author of *Secrets from a Country Kitchen*, also published by Ebury.

BIG THANK YOUS

Firstly of course to my lovely friend Mary Berry who has written such a wonderful foreword for this book. After seventeen years of working together we are still a team and with her amazing encouragement and support this is my third book. Mary, I can't thank you enough.

Big thanks too to Lucinda Kaizik who has helped me test the recipes and is a treasure to work with. Lucinda helps me with my demonstrations too and is the best assistant around – huge thanks, I couldn't do it without you. Thanks too to Judy Bicknell who checked for mistakes, of which there were a few! Thanks Jude.

This book would not have happened without the dedication and belief of Carey Smith at Ebury Press, always on my side and determined to get this book on the shelves, believing in my passion – thank you so much, Carey. Sarah Lavelle has been an absolute pleasure to work with too; I am lucky to have Ebury as my publishers. Also thanks to Emma Callery who edited the book with such precision, making sure everything reads correctly, and to Tony Lyons for his beautiful design. Thanks too to Michele Topham at Felicity Bryan, fantastic agents, answering every query with a smile. To Dawn Roads, Laura James and the team at Aga for their unreserved support. The delicious photos are down to Will Heap and Alice Hart; thank you for turning my recipes into mouth-watering pictures.

Finally, my family and friends, who have been with me every step of the way. This book has been a real challenge, but I have enjoyed every moment, and with every hug a new recipe was written.